HOMECOMING

HOME COMING

LEEANN MINOGUE

Homecoming
first published 2010 by
Scirocco Drama
An imprint of J. Gordon Shillingford Publishing Inc.

Scirocco Drama Editor: Glenda MacFarlane
Cover design by Terry Gallagher/Doowah Design Inc.
Author photo by Brad Barlow
Printed and bound in Canada on 100% post-consumer recycled paper.

We acknowledge the financial support of the Manitoba Arts Council, The Canada Council for the Arts and the Government of Canada through the Book Publishing Industry Development Program (BPIDP) for our publishing program.

Production inquiries should be addressed to:
Leeann Minogue
Box 56
Griffin, SK S0C 1G0

Library and Archives Canada Cataloguing in Publication

Minogue, Leeann, 1970-
Homecoming / Leeann Minogue.

A play.
ISBN 978-1-897289-49-5

I. Title.

PS8626.I56H64 2010 C811′.6 C2010-901724-2

J. Gordon Shillingford Publishing
P.O. Box 86, RPO Corydon Avenue, Winnipeg, MB Canada R3M 3S3

Acknowledgements

This play would not exist without Stephen Heatley. Stephen not only directed this show at the Station Arts Centre in Rosthern, he also helped to get this play on stage, he gave advice about rewrites, he facilitated a workshop in his own home in the early stages of development, and he talked me down from the metaphorical ledge at that point in the process when I was ready to give up writing altogether.

I am also grateful for: the cast of the Rosthern production who faced a new draft every day of rehearsals; helpful friends who took time to read and comment on drafts of the play; family and friends who went to see the show; my parents, who let me stay with them during rehearsals and are my biggest fans; and, of course, Brad and Matthew who make it possible.

Leeann Minogue

Leeann Minogue lives on a grain farm in south-eastern Saskatchewan with her husband Brad and their three-year old son Matthew. *Homecoming* is her second full-length play. *Dry Streak* (Scirocco Drama, 2006), her first play, was nominated for a Saskatchewan Book Award in 2006 and has been produced at the Persephone Theatre in Saskatoon, the Station Arts Centre in Rosthern, and the Grand Theatre in London, Ontario as well as 17 community dinner theatres across Saskatchewan.

Besides writing plays Leeann spends time with Matthew, helps out on the farm, writes articles for agricultural publications and continues to look for creative new ways to avoid housework.

Production History

Homecoming premiered at the Station Arts Centre in Rosthern, Saskatchewan in July, 2009 with the following cast:

MARLENE Wilson.. Sharon Bakker

NORMA Janson..Cynthia Dyck

GREG Wilson..Matt Josdal

JERRY Wilson ....Rob Roy

SUSAN Bryant.. Tara Schoonbaert

Directed by Stephen Heatley

Assistant Director: Brian Cochrane

Set Design by Hans Becker

Costume Design by Theresa Germain

Technical Work by Craig Langlois

Lighting Design by Lauchlin Johnston

Stage Manager: Diana Domm

Theatre Chairperson: Kathy Thiessen

Characters

Jerry Wilson.................................... retiring farmer, early 60s

Marlene Wilson .... Jerry's wife, early 60s

Greg Wilson .... 35, Jerry and Marlene's son

Susan Bryant .... 31, Jerry and Marlene's daughter

Norma Janson .... friend of Marlene

Setting

This play is set on the Wilson farm in June of 2005. The Wilson family farm is a grain farm, a few miles south of Stony Valley, Saskatchewan.

There are two locations:

* *Jerry's shop*: This is the space where Jerry keeps his tools and some small farm machinery. He spends a lot of time working in his shop, summer and winter. It could be represented by a simple workspace with a few tools. Part of the shop is offstage—characters can enter the shop from the door, or from the rest of the shop. On most farms, the shop would be a short walk from the house.

* *The Wilson farmhouse*: Jerry built this house 37 years ago (in 1968), when he and Marlene were first married. On stage, there is a living room and a dining room table. There is a phone in the living room. There are exits to the kitchen, to the outside, and to the 'rest of the house' (bedrooms and bathrooms).

Action moves between the two locations. The stage should be set to allow for quick scene changes between the two locations.

A Note About the Text

The use of the "/" symbol in the script indicates that the speaker is interrupted by the next line.

Act One

Scene 1

Wednesday, June 1, 2005.

Jerry's shop.

JERRY is alone, puttering in his shop, fixing an alternator from a truck or tractor on his workbench. It's a complicated job that requires a lot of concentration. He has a large cast or brace on his leg and walks using crutches. He's been using them for a few weeks, but he's still a bit clumsy.

JERRY: Geez… Got it… That Greg. Telling me I'd have to get this fixed at the dealership… Ha… I still know what I'm doing.

MARLENE: *(Offstage.)* Jerry! Jerry! It's almost two-thirty already.

JERRY: Hope this alternator keeps charging this time.

Scene 2

Immediately following.

The Wilson farmhouse.

Lights go out on the shop and come up on the living room, where MARLENE is surrounded by full packing boxes. There is only minimal furniture in the room—a couch, coffee table, an old macramé wall hanging. MARLENE is restlessly packing and unpacking a few final items and looking around the house, making sure nothing's been left behind. MARLENE checks her watch.

MARLENE: *(To herself.)* I can't believe this. *(She goes to the outside exit, opens it, leans out, and shouts.)* Jerry!

MARLENE closes the door and goes back to her packing.

(To herself.) Honestly.

JERRY comes in on his crutches, after some difficulty with the door.

Jerry, it's nearly two-thirty. Greg'll be here any second.

JERRY: Had to finish changing the bearings in the alternator.

JERRY takes a seat on the couch, and maneuvers his casted leg up onto the table.

MARLENE: Don't you think we have enough going on today? I could use some help in here.

JERRY: Help? I'm on crutches, you know.

MARLENE: Believe me. I know... Look, I've got almost everything all packed. There's just a few things left to deal with... What do you think about this old wall hanging?

JERRY: Huh?

MARLENE: I know it's old. But it fits that spot. What do you think?

JERRY: Marlene. I can barely go to the bathroom on my own. Couldn't put my own crop in the ground. Stumbling around on crutches for two months. And you ask me about a wall hanging?

MARLENE: This 'feeling sorry for yourself' routine is getting old.

JERRY: That's the pot calling the kettle slack. You're not getting any younger either.

MARLENE: Sixty isn't old anymore. It's the new forty-five.

JERRY: Wait until you lose your health.

MARLENE: Nobody forced you to ski down that black diamond run.

JERRY: Alec and Rick were egging me on. I couldn't just take a green run like an old man. What would the guys say?

MARLENE: I know what the Ski Patrol said: "They'd never seen anybody wrapped so tight around a tree."

JERRY: Those young hotshots were more worried about cracking jokes than my leg. I'm not sure it was broken before they came along.

MARLENE: Right.

JERRY: And it's not my fault it was icy. Darn spring skiing. Don't know why the guys couldn't go skiing in January, instead of drying up in the desert all winter.

MARLENE: Now that I'm retired, we could go to Arizona too. Lynn and the girls have so much fun. Golfing. Going to the flea markets.

JERRY: I can't leave the farm. There's wheat to haul. Canola to sell. This isn't a part-time hobby.

MARLENE: Things'll be different now. Greg'll be doing those things.

JERRY: That doesn't mean we need go and live like nomads in a trailer court.

MARLENE: Right. I think I'll just leave it here.

JERRY: What?

MARLENE: The wall hanging!

JERRY: Excuse me if I'm not focused on your decorations, Marlene. I'm leaving the place I've lived all my life. The house I built with my own two hands. I'm giving up everything.

MARLENE: Not everything, Jerry. I'm going with you, remember?

JERRY: Trust me, I remember.

MARLENE: Don't give me that, Jerry Wilson. I left my job two months early to help you with your leg. Before the end of the school year. Before the graduation! What kind of school secretary does that?

JERRY: I know. I know.

MARLENE: And look at Dave Reimer.

JERRY: What about him?

MARLENE: After Dave and Rhonda left their farm, they weren't living in town for two weeks before she packed up and left Dave. Off to go and live in a condo in Victoria with her new boyfriend.

JERRY: Oh, yeah. That vegetarian hippie she met at a yoga class in the city. I ask you Marlene—what kind of man teaches yoga?

MARLENE: You could have it worse, you know.

JERRY: I know. I know. But what am I gonna do in Stony Valley all day? Sit on the couch? Look out the window? Wait for the neighbour's dog take a dump on our lawn?

MARLENE: There'll be work to do on the new house.

JERRY: But I won't have my tools in town. Anyway, the timing's all wrong. I've got a good fifteen years left in me. Maybe Greg and Andrea could rent a place in Stony Valley for a while instead of moving in here right away.

MARLENE: Plans have been made, Jerry. Greg's quit his job in the city. We've bought a new house.

JERRY: But if we had more time to work things out… Maybe Greg and Andrea could just stay with us, here, in Greg's old room for a while.

MARLENE: And the four of us could eat every meal together, like some kind of Hutterite colony?

JERRY: Andrea's never spent any time on a farm. What if she doesn't like it here?

MARLENE: Andrea knows what she's getting into.

JERRY: You know everything about everybody, don't you?

MARLENE: I know this is hard for you, but you don't have to be mean.

JERRY: This is a big day.

MARLENE: Jerry Wilson. You've been planning for this day since Greg was born.

JERRY: What?

MARLENE: All the other new fathers brought flowers and teddy bears to the hospital. You came in with a three-foot John Deere riding tractor.

JERRY: Every farmer wants his son to take over the farm.

MARLENE: And that's what's happening.

JERRY: But it's too soon. If I hadn't broken my damn leg…

MARLENE: You'd hang on to this farm until we pried your cold dead hands off the steering wheel of the combine… Greg's thirty-five. He's ready.

JERRY: You don't understand. In this business there's no room for mistakes.

MARLENE: Relax. The crop looks great this year.

JERRY: It's only the first of June, Marlene. Anything could happen before we get it in the bin. Hail. Drought. A flood.

MARLENE: Oh Jerry.

JERRY: Farming is risky. Fertilizer bills. Chemical bills. If Greg's not careful, he could lose everything.

MARLENE: Greg's ready. He learned a lot at the university. And then doing that job for the last eight years.

JERRY: Some job. Government agrologist.

MARLENE: And he's been listening to you all his life.

JERRY: Just until I take a breath. Then he badgers me about some new idea.

MARLENE: Jerry, this is Greg's chance. We have to let him take it. We're retiring. Together.

JERRY: Maybe we can go to the dentist together too.

MARLENE: I'll ask you one more time. Do you think I should leave this old hanging here for Greg and Andrea?

JERRY: That's your department.

There's a knock on the door.

MARLENE: That'll be Greg.

JERRY: I guess this is the end.

MARLENE: Or the beginning. *(Calling out the door.)* Come on in, Greg.

GREG enters.

GREG: That canola north of the house sure looks great.

MARLENE: Hello Greg.

JERRY acknowledges GREG with a nod.

GREG: Oh good. You've got everything all packed up.

JERRY: Yep. Ready to get to town.

MARLENE: Almost… There's a bit of a holdup.

JERRY: What?

MARLENE: *(To GREG.)* Your sister still has a few things to clear out of her old bedroom.

GREG: Oh. Whatever. Susan'll get to it when she has time.

MARLENE: No. It's not right. You and Andrea need a fresh start here. You can't have Susan popping in and out looking for her things.

GREG: I doubt she'd drive out from Stony Valley to see her old Duran Duran posters that often.

MARLENE: And you two might want to use that room for something else.

GREG: Yeah. Andrea was saying something about an office.

MARLENE: I guess Susan will get out here when she's done marking all the students' essays… But I think she's a little put out.

JERRY: What do you mean?

MARLENE: She comes out here a lot, when Scott's busy. She still thinks of this place as home.

JERRY: That's silly. She's a married woman.

MARLENE: Yes, but she's still close to her family. She needs our support.

JERRY: Then she shouldn't have married a band teacher, Marlene. Especially one with a chihuahua. I'm surprised she took her nose out of a book long enough to even know we're moving.

MARLENE: Oh Jerry. Just be kind to her, will you?

JERRY: Yeah, yeah. *(To GREG.)* Got all your stuff out in the truck?

GREG: The worst of it, anyway. Andrea's clothes. You wouldn't believe how many shoes that woman has.

JERRY: A woman without shoes is like a fish without lemon juice.

MARLENE: Has Andrea picked out new furniture for this place yet?

GREG: Don't think so.

MARLENE: Oh good. Maybe I can help out. I don't know much about decorating, but I did notice some things that would fit in here when I was re-doing the teachers' lounge this winter.

JERRY: Let the kids pick out their own things, Marlene.

MARLENE: I thought looking at furniture would be something Andrea and I could do together.

GREG: I'm sure Andrea would like that.

MARLENE: Andrea! Where is she? She's not out unpacking the truck? You need a break from the drive before we start moving boxes.

GREG: Andrea couldn't come with me. She got a last minute job interview this afternoon. She'll bring her car out later.

JERRY: Job interview? In the city?

GREG: Yeah. Same place she's been working—different department. They might let her work part time, or from home, or something.

MARLENE: I thought she was looking forward to taking the summer off.

JERRY: It's a ninety minute drive to the city! With gas almost a dollar a litre—making that drive every day would cost a fortune!

GREG: She won't drive in every day, Dad. And there's not a lot of jobs out here in Stony Valley.

MARLENE: No. Did you know they're closing the school unit office? Four people are losing their jobs.

JERRY: Darn government. First the hospitals. Then the schools. The only thing those politicians care about outside the city is the property tax on our farmland.

MARLENE: I hope she doesn't get too busy with a job. I'm looking forward to spending time with her. Now that I'm retired.

GREG: Don't worry. She'll want to spend some time with you.

MARLENE: Do you think she'll be here on Thursday night?

GREG: Probably. Why?

MARLENE: The Homecoming Committee's having a meeting.

GREG: What's that?

JERRY: Come on. It's 2005. Saskatchewan centennial. Stony Valley Homecoming. Every town from Avonlea to Zealandia's having some kind of shindig. Don't you read *The Stony Valley Review*?

MARLENE: There's a big do here on the July first weekend, Greg. A pancake breakfast, slo-pitch tournament. That kind of thing. And a big Friday night barbeque to kick things off.

GREG: Sounds like a lot of planning.

MARLENE: Norma Janson's struck up a committee of ladies. We have a month left to plan.

GREG: You're on the committee?

MARLENE: Oh, not you too.

JERRY: Ha! I told you nobody would forget what happened when you tried to join the church choir last winter.

MARLENE: Norma's not the only one who knows about music.

GREG: Norma asked you to join her Committee?

MARLENE: Yes. She left a message on our answering machine, saying she could use my help, now that I'll have more time. And I'm willing to forgive and forget.

GREG: So you forgot about that time you subbed on Norma's rink in the Ladies' Bonspiel?

MARLENE: I probably should have kept my mouth shut. But I was the third. I was supposed to help her call the shots. She shouldn't've got so mad.

GREG: The guys watching from the bar had a pool going on which one of you would hit the ice first.

MARLENE: Oh, they did not.

JERRY: I hope this Homecoming Committee doesn't turn out like that. I could barely live with you for weeks after that bonspiel.

MARLENE: Norma and I are adults. We used to be close, back

when we both had young kids… I'll go to the meetings and do what she tells me to do. This is her project. I'll just be a quiet worker bee.

GREG: She'd better watch out for your stinger.

MARLENE: I'll keep busy at the meetings making sure Andrea gets to know everyone.

JERRY: If Andrea wants to be on the Committee.

GREG: Andrea's looking forward to doing things out here. Getting to know everybody. She says, "If you're going to make a change, you have to jump in with both feet."

JERRY starts hobbling around, getting ready to try to lift boxes.

JERRY: So I guess it's just the three of us moving all this stuff.

MARLENE: Jerry, stop that.

GREG: Don't be crazy. Sit down.

JERRY: I hope you don't think your mother's going to move all these boxes.

GREG: Relax. I stopped in Stony Valley on my way out from the city. Tim and Darren are coming out to give us a hand.

MARLENE: Oh that's a relief.

JERRY hobbles back to the couch.

JERRY: Humph. We could've done it ourselves. Everybody in town'll be thinking I'm too feeble to haul my own stuff around.

MARLENE: I'll go and mix up some lemonade for your friends. It's a warm day. And I think there's some of those good muffins from Costco in the freezer.

JERRY: It's not your kitchen anymore, Marlene. And I thought you cleaned it out.

MARLENE: I couldn't leave them out here with empty cupboards.

GREG: Don't worry Dad. I don't care who does what in the kitchen.

JERRY: Your wife might.

GREG: We'll worry about that when she gets here.

MARLENE exits to the kitchen.

JERRY: I think your mother's having a little trouble getting used to the idea of moving to town. It can be hard for some people to get used to new things.

GREG: Oh?

JERRY: Whatdaya mean by that?

GREG: Nothing.

JERRY: Is this about that GIS thing again?

GREG: GPS. Global Positioning System.

JERRY: I've been steering the tractor by myself for forty-four years. And those GIS things are dangerous. Look what happened to John Richards.

GREG: Even John should've known better than to let the GPS steer while he sat on the tractor steps eating his lunch.

JERRY: If the thing's supposed to steer, might as well let it steer.

GREG: It does more than steer.

JERRY: Sounds like a lot of money for a bunch of maps.

GREG: The maps'll show where I can use less fertilizer. It'll pay for itself in no time.

JERRY: I've heard that before.

GREG: Once you see the yield maps I get off the combine you'll understand.

JERRY: Whoa, wait a minute.

GREG: What? The maps show all kinds of /

JERRY: Not the maps. The combine.

GREG: What about it?

JERRY: You might be taking over the farm, but that doesn't mean you're taking over my seat on the combine.

GREG: What?

JERRY: You're still gonna need help out here during harvest. I'll still be running the combine.

GREG: Dad I thought when I /

JERRY: Think about this. I've been running the combine since I took over this farm from my father.

GREG: Exactly.

JERRY: Exactly! *(Pause.)* ...Oh... Yeah. I see what you mean. Shit... Ah geez. Well, yeah. I guess you'll be the foreman. But I don't know how much time I'll have to help out. I'll have a lot of stuff to do in town.

GREG: Sure.

JERRY: Yeah. Geez... I took a close look at the basement of the new house yesterday. Gonna have to repaint the whole thing. That damn Jeff Murphy. Guy must've let his dog paint the place. Didn't even take the baseboards off. Don't know why I bought a house from that guy.

GREG: It's a good house.

JERRY: Poor investment. Susan's band-teaching husband

gave me a big lecture about that. House prices aren't going anywhere. The government can pay for all the Centennial parties they want, but I don't see a bunch of moving vans lining up in small town Saskatchewan.

GREG: Whattaya mean? There's a truck full of boxes right in your driveway.

JERRY: Smartass.

Scene 3

Two weeks later. Tuesday, June 14, 2005, evening.

Jerry's shop.

GREG is in the shop, by himself, tinkering with something.

MARLENE: *(Calling from offstage.)* Greg? Greg?

GREG: *(Calling loudly.)* In the shop Mom.

MARLENE enters the shop, carrying some Tupperware.

MARLENE: I stopped by the house, but nobody was there. You're still working?

GREG: Andrea's not home yet. Thought I might as well finish this up.

MARLENE: Not home? It's after nine.

GREG: She'll be home any minute. She called around seven-thirty and said she was leaving the city right away.

MARLENE: Good. She's been so busy since you moved in, I'm sure she hasn't had time to bake.

GREG: It's only been two weeks.

MARLENE: I know. I brought you a carrot cake.

GREG: Wow. Thanks. That's my favorite.

MARLENE: I know. I was in the city today—picking up supplies for the Homecoming Committee, and I thought of you when I saw this at Costco.

GREG: Andrea won't buy it for me. She says the cream cheese icing's too fattening.

MARLENE: She's right.

GREG: Thanks Mom. Want a piece?

MARLENE: I'd better not. I've been eating way too much lately. I just can't stop myself.

GREG: Oh?

MARLENE: I don't have enough to do. Spending all day in the house. With the fridge.

GREG: I thought you had lots of plans.

MARLENE: Oh, I do. It's just strange, waking up in the morning and not having anywhere to be. The house is so quiet. And your dad's usually out here all day. I'm used to the school, with lots of people around. But don't worry about me. I'll get into the swing of things.

GREG: You're busy with the Homecoming plans?

MARLENE: Oh yes. Norma's got us marching along to her tune.

GREG: Someone has to be in charge.

MARLENE: I suppose.

GREG: You could just tell Norma you're not interested.

MARLENE: I'm not letting Norma get the better of me. And I'm going to have to deal with her sooner or later. She's got her hand in everything. The library board. The school board. The kitchen at the rec centre.

GREG: You'll manage. If you could cope with all those teachers and students, you'll get through this.

MARLENE: I hope you're right. But keeping three hundred students in line is easier than keeping my mouth shut with Hurricane Norma at the helm of a two-hour meeting... Greg, don't tell anyone I've been talking like this. Especially your father. I don't want him to think I can't handle retiring.

GREG: Of course not.

MARLENE: There's no point making him more crazy than he already is... And are you OK? You and Andrea? Do you think living out here is going to work out for the two of you?

GREG: Yeah. Andrea likes it here. I'm not so sure about Dad though.

MARLENE: Andrea doesn't like your father?

GREG: No, no. Not that. It's just... Well... Geez Mom. He's been out here every day this week.

MARLENE: I noticed that... He knows better... He tells me you need the help.

GREG: I appreciate the help. But geez. He's gotta stop telling me what to do.

MARLENE: That's just his way. He knows what he's doing.

GREG: So do I. I've made a living giving farmers advice for eight years now.

MARLENE: Your father's having a hard time letting go. This farm is everything to him.

GREG: I love the farm too. But he's driving me nuts. He was nagging me about the way I set the welder the other day. I've taken six welding classes in the city. I wanted to storm out of the shop and drive right back to my old apartment. Leave him here to do the work himself. With his broken leg.

MARLENE: You're not going to do that.

GREG: No. Of course not.

MARLENE: I know you and your father are a bit rough on each other sometimes. But try to keep cool, will you? Until he settles into retirement. Things will work out.

GREG: I guess you're right... Where is Dad anyway? You didn't leave him home by himself, did you?

MARLENE: He's at a Masons meeting.

GREG: Masons? With the secret handshakes, and the goats and the DaVinci Code and everything? I didn't know Dad was a Mason.

MARLENE: He's always been a Mason.

SUSAN enters.

SUSAN: Who's always been a Mason?

GREG: Hey Susan.

MARLENE: Your father's a Mason.

SUSAN: What? I've read about Masons, but I had no idea we had one in the family.

GREG: Guess he's pretty good at keeping those Mason secrets.

MARLENE: He hasn't had time to go the meetings for the last few years. Not since you two were babies and he needed an excuse to get out of the house.

GREG: Huh. Who knew?

SUSAN: Not me. As usual.

MARLENE: What're you up to tonight Susan?

SUSAN: I came to pick up another box of my books.

MARLENE: You still haven't got that room cleaned out?

SUSAN: I'm almost done. It's not like I've had a lot of notice. I guess I should just be glad you remembered to tell me Greg was moving in…instead of just throwing all my stuff out in the ditch.

MARLENE: Come on Susan. You know we wouldn't do that.

GREG: I'd leave it on the lawn.

MARLENE: Greg.

GREG: I'm just kidding.

SUSAN: I just wish I knew what was going on around here. I care about this place. Even if I'm not married to a farmer.

GREG: What? Scott's not a farmer?

MARLENE: Greg, you're not helping. Susan, you'll always be part of this family.

SUSAN: The part that's getting kicked out of my own bedroom.

MARLENE: You haven't lived here in years.

GREG: It's not like you and Scott are sleeping under a bridge.

SUSAN: We might as well be, living in that dingy old duplex.

MARLENE: That's your choice.

SUSAN: There's hardly any place to rent in Stony Valley.

MARLENE: You and Scott are both teachers with good salaries. You could buy any house in town.

SUSAN: Scott says it makes more sense to rent, and put our money in the stock market instead of a house. He told Dad that before you bought your place. But Dad never listens to Scott… And it's not like I have time to pack up everything from my childhood. I'm still at the school every day, even if you're not.

MARLENE: Trust me. Keeping the principal from strapping the Murphy twins was a picnic next to looking after your father when he has a sore leg.

SUSAN: I have a husband to look after too. And a dog. Buffy's not going to feed and walk herself while I sort through all my old baby clothes. I've got lots of things to do besides hang around here.

GREG: Do you want me to move some of your boxes?

SUSAN: Maybe. But I don't know where I'm going to put everything. There's hardly any room in the duplex. With Scott's music stands and speakers and all of Buffy's things…

GREG: You can stash things here in the shop. There's some room over in that corner. *(Points offstage.)* With our camping stuff and those old bookshelves.

SUSAN: You wouldn't mind? I won't be taking up too much of your space?

GREG: You might want to pick up a few of those big Rubbermaid boxes. Unless you don't mind a few mice crawling through your old legwarmers and cassette tapes.

SUSAN: At least there's no mice in the duplex.

GREG: See? Now you're happy to be kicked out of here.

SUSAN: Don't make fun. Nothing's changing for you.

GREG: My whole life's changing!

SUSAN: But you're right back in the house where you grew up. I have to move all my stuff around like a homeless person. I don't even know where I'm going to have Christmas dinner.

GREG: Christmas? It's June!

MARLENE: We'll have Christmas at the new place in town.

SUSAN: It won't be the same.

MARLENE: Of course it will. We'll be the same people eating the same food.

GREG: That same old green jelly salad in the same old green bowl.

SUSAN: Grandma always made that. You just pretend not to like it.

MARLENE: Well it's easy to make.

SUSAN: Never mind Christmas. I barely even see you anymore, now that you're not at the school.

MARLENE: I'm right in town Susan. You can come by anytime you like.

SUSAN: The new place isn't home… And anyway, you know how busy it is for teachers at the end of the school year.

MARLENE: Yes, I know… How are things at the school?

SUSAN: Alright. The kids have written some good essays.

MARLENE: And what about the new secretary? Is she working out?

SUSAN: I guess. She's got new ideas about next year's schedules. Scott says all the teachers are going to hate it.

MARLENE: New schedules? Oh my.

SUSAN: I'd better get going. Scott'll be wondering where I am. And Buffy'll need to go out.

MARLENE: Maybe we could get together on Saturday. You could tell me more about these new schedules.

SUSAN: I can't. We're going to the city.

MARLENE: Oh?

SUSAN: Scott's taking the school jazz band in for a competition. And he says Buffy likes that new dog park on the south end.

MARLENE: Well you have a good time.

GREG: You can pick up some of those rubber containers.

SUSAN: I might.

SUSAN leaves.

MARLENE: Well, it's getting late. I should get out of your way. I don't want Andrea to catch me babying you.

GREG: Thanks for the cake.

MARLENE: Anytime, Greg. All you have to do is ask.

GREG: What? I'm gonna have to start asking?

MARLENE: I should've made sure Susan had her things cleaned out sooner. But you know how she is. All wrapped up in her own life. School. Scott. And that stupid chihuahua.

GREG: Don't worry about it Mom.

GREG starts trying to get back to work.

MARLENE: Susan's not taking this change very well. It's almost as hard for her as it is for her father. And I don't know what those teachers are going to think about new schedules...

GREG: Yeah.

MARLENE: The lawn's sure green with all that rain… I guess I'd better go…

MARLENE leaves and GREG goes back to work.

GREG: Tough for a guy to get any work done around here.

Scene 4

The following morning—Wednesday, June 15, 2005.

The Wilson farmhouse.

There is no one in the house. The boxes are gone and there are a few of GREG's things out. The wall hanging MARLENE worried about earlier is gone. JERRY limps in from outside with his crutches, exhausted and rumpled. He leans against the wall, then makes his way to a chair. GREG enters and is surprised to see JERRY.

GREG: What the heck are you doing here?

JERRY: Only two weeks since I moved out and I can't even drop by?

GREG: You're here every day. You just surprised me. How'd you get here? Your truck's not in the driveway.

JERRY: Your mom dropped me off.

GREG: I would've seen her drive in.

JERRY: OK, OK, I walked.

GREG: Walked? Five miles? From town? On crutches?

JERRY: Two miles. From the Richards' place.

GREG: The Richards' place? What were you doing there?

JERRY: Having a coffee.

GREG: They're twenty years younger than you. And doesn't John have a job in town? He wouldn't even be home at this time of the morning.

JERRY: Well…

GREG: Look Dad, I know moving to town's been really hard for you. But you can't just go wandering around the country, dropping in for coffee whenever /

JERRY: Alright. Alright. I wasn't there for coffee.

GREG: Then what's going on?

JERRY: Ah shit… I went downtown. For a walk. And I saw your mom's SUV parked in front of the post office. I couldn't figure out what she was doing there.

GREG: Getting the mail, maybe?

JERRY: That's the point. I got the mail first thing this morning, like always. I watched her look through it. She didn't need to get the mail.

GREG: Maybe she was mailing something.

JERRY: But what? And why not just get me to take it in? She was up to something.

GREG: What?

JERRY: I don't know! That's the whole point! She's sneaking around behind my back, mailing things, or picking things up. Maybe she's got her own post office box. Maybe she's getting mail from a stranger.

GREG: How would she get mail from a stranger?

JERRY: Dave Reimer's wife probably got lots of mail from strangers—before she took off for the coast.

GREG: Don't be crazy. Mom's not going anywhere.

JERRY: That's what Dave Reimer thought.

GREG: What does this have to do with you walking here from the Richards' place?

JERRY: Your mother was up to something at the post office, so I wanted to see where she'd go next.

GREG: And?

JERRY: So I snuck into the back of her SUV and hid behind the seat. And waited until she got back in.

GREG: Where'd she go? Behind the Co-op to shoot heroin? Over to the bus depot to pick up some illegal aliens?

JERRY: She drove out of town! I couldn't figure out where she was going.

GREG: Maybe out here?

JERRY: That's what I thought. Until she went right by this place and turned at the five-mile corner.

GREG: What?

JERRY: I was down behind the seat, trying to figure out what she was doing. Then when I started looking around, there was a kid's car seat in front of me.

GREG: A car seat.

JERRY: And a bunch of toys on the floor, under my feet.

GREG: Oh no.

JERRY: So I peeked up over the seat, and—can you believe it? There was Kate Richards behind the wheel.

GREG: Oh Dad. The wrong SUV.

JERRY: It's not my fault if they all look alike. Damn car salesmen shouldn't sell everybody in town the same colour SUV.

GREG: What did Kate say? Did you talk her out of calling the cops.

JERRY: I wasn't going to talk to her. For God's sake. She'd think I was some kind of nut.

GREG: You think?

JERRY: So I waited until she got her groceries and went into the house. Then I snuck out the side door of the garage and down to the road.

GREG: Oh God.

JERRY: I'm sure she didn't see me. Her kitchen faces the other side of the yard.

GREG: But didn't anybody see you hobbling down the road? Somebody should've stopped and given you a ride.

JERRY: Don't be stupid. I wasn't going to let anybody see me! I hid in the ditch every time a car came by. That's why it took me so damn long to get here.

GREG: Oh God.

MARLENE knocks at the door, and then enters without waiting for an answer.

MARLENE: Greg? Greg? Has your father… *(She sees JERRY.)* Oh! Here you are.

GREG: How'd you know he was here?

MARLENE: Kate Richards called. She saw you sneaking in and out of her SUV. She wanted to make sure you were alright.

JERRY: Oh geez.

MARLENE: She said you walked all the way here. Are you OK?

JERRY: I'm fine. And I don't want to talk about it.

MARLENE: But what were you doing?

JERRY: Never mind. *(To GREG.)* Don't just stand around snickering. Get me a cup of coffee.

GREG: I've got some on.

GREG exits for the kitchen to make coffee.

MARLENE: You were trying to follow me around town, weren't you? You thought that was my SUV… Where did you think I would go?

JERRY: Rhonda Reimer found plenty of places to go, didn't she?

MARLENE: You thought maybe I was taking some yoga classes at the post office?

JERRY: Well…

MARLENE: Or sending away for a mail order lesson? It's a good thing you don't know where I actually was.

JERRY: Where were you?

MARLENE: I was at Stephenson's store. You've really got to find something to do.

JERRY: I've got plenty to do.

MARLENE: Sure you do. Oh, hey. You really do have something to do. Alec called while you were…"out".

JERRY: What'd he want?

MARLENE: The Elks are meeting tonight. He was wondering if you'd go.

JERRY: Elks? Geez. It's bad enough I have to go to the darn Mason meetings.

MARLENE: There's nothing wrong with the Elks. They raise lots of money for good causes.

JERRY: Hmph. Bunch of old guys. Gums flapping in the breeze while they solve the world's problems. Talk, talk, talk.

MARLENE: You might as well get used to it. That's what retired people do. They spend time together.

JERRY: Like we're doing now? I could pass.

MARLENE pauses for a minute and looks around the room.

MARLENE: Andrea's taken down my wall hanging.

JERRY: Huh?

MARLENE: Do you think she put it up somewhere else?

JERRY: Never mind Marlene. It's not your house anymore.

MARLENE: I'm just curious. I made that hanging, you know. She could give it back to me if she doesn't like it. I wonder where she put it.

GREG enters from the kitchen, carrying coffee.

GREG: Where who put what?

JERRY: Never mind. Nothing. Your mother's having trouble adjusting to living in town.

MARLENE: And you're setting a shining example for everyone. *(To GREG.)* I was just wondering about the wall hanging I left in the living room.

GREG: I wouldn't know anything about that. You'll have to ask Andrea.

MARLENE: I will when I see her. She's been so busy these last two weeks.

GREG: Her new job's hectic right now.

MARLENE: As long as she's happy. It's too bad she's missed the last couple of Homecoming Committee meetings, though.

GREG: Wasn't she at one last week?

MARLENE: Sort of. She got there late, on her way home from work. We were all on our way out the door when she was coming in.

GREG: That's too bad.

MARLENE: I'll say. Those meetings would be more fun if I had someone there to commiserate with.

JERRY: Commiserate?

MARLENE: Oh you know Norma. When she's not letting everyone rattle on and on she's telling us what to do. She's sneaky. And I'm just not used to working with so many women. I've organized the entire Stony Valley Grade 12 Graduation single-handedly since 1989. But a big committee takes forever to get anything done.

JERRY: Too many cooks can broil a sloth.

MARLENE: And with Andrea missing so many meetings, those women think she doesn't care about the Homecoming.

JERRY: Oh boy. Don't let Norma and the rest of those women start gossiping all over town about Andrea, or we'll look like idiots.

GREG: Why do you care what they think?

JERRY: Why don't you?… She's not just your wife.

GREG: What?

JERRY: She's a Wilson now. Part of the Wilson farm. We've been building a reputation for generations—we can't have some new wife of yours ruining it in a month.

MARLENE: Jerry.

GREG: Are you kidding?

JERRY: No. I'm not.

GREG: Andrea's not ruining anything. She's been nice to everybody out here.

JERRY: When she's been here.

GREG: She's working. If she didn't have a job you'd complain about that too.

JERRY: What people think is important. And since we're on the subject, Andrea's really letting that garden go. You can see the weeds from the road.

MARLENE: Enough, Jerry. I'll give her a hand.

JERRY: It looks like a tornado drove through it, but it's not your garden Marlene. This is Andrea's yard now. You've got your own garden in town.

MARLENE: It's a flower pot.

GREG: Andrea will get to the garden.

MARLENE: I'd just like to help. I have time, and I'm the one who planted all the vegetables out there.

JERRY: If they want your help, they'll ask for it Marlene.

MARLENE: *(To JERRY.)* After all your griping. I'm trying to pitch in. Make things easier for her. You're the one who's been complaining that Andrea's not committed enough to the farm.

JERRY: I didn't say that

MARLENE: Oh oh.

GREG: Andrea's not "committed enough"? She's packed everything up. Changed jobs. Moved out here. What else do you want?

JERRY: She's not spending much time out here.

GREG: She's catching up at her new job.

JERRY: She's got some catching up to do here, too. That's all I'm saying.

GREG: I think you've said too much.

MARLENE: We've all said too much. Let's go home Jerry. We'd better find something to do in town.

JERRY: I'm not going to town Marlene. I've gotta help Greg. That's the problem with a heavy crop. We've gotta find room to put it all. We've gotta clean out some bins.

MARLENE: Oh for heaven's sake. What did you just tell me about the garden?

JERRY: This is different. This is a two-man job. Do you want everybody in town thinking I'm too old to shovel wheat?

MARLENE: You're on crutches. And you've had enough exercise for one day.

JERRY: I'm not some old man.

MARLENE: You don't really want me driving my SUV around town all by myself, do you? What if I wind up at an exercise class?

JERRY: The kid's got a farm to run and he needs my help.

GREG: Whatever. Let's just get at it. I've got a lot of stuff to do today.

JERRY: See, Marlene?

As GREG and JERRY head for the door, there is a knock.

GREG: There's the cops. They're hunting down the stalker.

JERRY: Nobody called the cops.

MARLENE: Come in.

NORMA opens the door and peeks around it before entering.

NORMA: Oh! You're all here.

GREG: Good morning Norma.

JERRY: Hello Norma.

MARLENE: Why don't you come on in?

NORMA: Are you sure? I don't want to get in the way. I really just came to see Andrea.

MARLENE: She's not here, but since you've come all the way out here, you might as well have a cup of coffee. We can talk about the Homecoming.

NORMA: Well, I just dropped in on my way back from the garbage dump. I've got a luncheon meeting, but I guess I could stop in for a minute or two.

MARLENE: Greg's got some coffee on. I'll just get you some.

NORMA: Andrea doesn't mind you in her kitchen when she's not home?

GREG: Nah. Don't worry about that. *(Aside to JERRY.)* Unless they start breaking the good dishes.

NORMA: Well, alright then. *(To JERRY.)* How are you liking the new house? I heard there was a moving truck full of new furniture at your place last week.

JERRY: Yep. Greg's buying new stuff for this place too. My broken leg's been a great excuse for everybody to get new furniture.

MARLENE: We needed new things.

JERRY: Without the old couch, I'm the oldest thing in the

house. If I don't watch out Marlene'll trade me in for a new model. Someone that goes better with the curtains.

MARLENE: Or someone that can stand on his head.

NORMA: You sure seem to be taking this well. So many men have such a hard time handing over the farm.

JERRY: Nothing to worry about here. Greg knows what he's doing. The Wilson farm's in good hands.

NORMA: And your wife seems like a real nice girl, Greg.

JERRY: She sure is.

NORMA: I only spent a few minutes with her at the Committee meeting last week. She was in such a rush.

GREG: She'll have more time once her new job settles down.

NORMA: Then she'll be busy again, once Jerry and Marlene get some grandchildren. I have two already, you know.

GREG: I'd better get to work.

Both men head for the door.

I'll have Andrea give you a call tonight.

NORMA: Thanks Greg. And maybe I'll see you Jerry…out taking a stroll on the highway.

JERRY: Ah geez.

MARLENE: Oh dear.

JERRY and GREG leave.

Have a chair. I'll get the coffee.

NORMA: That sounds good.

MARLENE goes to the kitchen and comes back with

two mugs. They continue the conversation while she's in the other room, with MARLENE calling out from offstage.

MARLENE: You still drink yours black?

NORMA: You remember? It's been a long time.

MARLENE: Yes.

NORMA: But I guess you have a lot of time these days. And Jerry too, obviously. He's even crazier than usual now that he's moved to town.

MARLENE: I wouldn't say that.

NORMA: Really? Following you around town?

MARLENE: Well…

NORMA: Spending every waking moment out here, bothering Greg.

MARLENE: Greg can use the help.

NORMA: Greg? He's been ready to run this farm since he was six.

MARLENE: Passing a family business on to the next generation is always tricky. You're so lucky you never had to do that.

NORMA: Our Shane had more sense than to want to farm. He's got a great career out in Vancouver.

MARLENE: Oh, he's found another job then? I'm so glad. Too bad he didn't get the kids after that divorce.

NORMA: I'm surprised you had time to pay attention.

MARLENE: Why would you say that?

NORMA: You haven't had time for me in years. The only reason you're sitting down with me today is because you're bored without your precious job.

MARLNE: Norma Janson /

NORMA: Yep. As soon as Susan was old enough to get her own after-school snack out of a box you were off in town, creating your own empire in the school office.

MARLENE: But /

NORMA: And I was just one of the little people left behind in your wake. All by myself on the farm. With Leonard. And the cows.

MARLENE: I made time /

NORMA: For your garden and your yard. There I was, after Leonard died, arranging the farm auction all by myself. Buying a house. Moving to town.

MARLENE: But /

NORMA: And then one day you finally did come by. You came to sell raffle tickets for the school grad.

MARLENE: Norma /

NORMA: But never mind. Olive Richards talked me into being head of the rink kitchen that first winter I was in town. I was shy /

MARLENE: I'd forgotten how quiet you used to be.

NORMA: But Olive was there to help me. And I learned the ropes from her.

MARLENE: And now you're practically running the town.

NORMA: Is that what they say?

MARLENE: Well, yes. They do.

NORMA: Hmmm.

MARLENE: And now I'm the one looking for something to do.

NORMA: Interesting isn't it? ...And speaking of interesting, what did Kate say when she realized Jerry was lurking in the back of her Ford Explorer?

MARLENE: You didn't see him out on the highway, did you?

NORMA: No. Eileen called me from the post office.

Scene 5

The same day—late afternoon.

Jerry's shop.

GREG is working in the shop, but offstage, with the radio playing in the background. JERRY enters from outside and looks around, irritated, and shuts the music off.

JERRY: Darn music. A guy can hardly hear himself think with this stuff playing.

GREG enters from inside the shop, holding a wrench, wiping off dust and grime.

GREG: What're you doing?

JERRY: I don't know how you can work out here, with that music playing.

GREG: I like a little background noise.

JERRY: A job worth doing is another man's poison... What're you doing to the tractor?

GREG: Replacing the clutch.

JERRY: The clutch? That clutch was fine the last time I used the tractor. That machine's not even four years old.

GREG: It's starting to slip a bit when it pulls hard.

JERRY: You're spending money like you're the Bill Gates of Stony Valley.

GREG: I'm doing it myself so there's no labour costs. It won't come to much more than fifteen hundred dollars.

JERRY: What? For a clutch that doesn't even need replacing?

GREG: You have to spend money to make money. And the crops look great.

JERRY: Your grandfather would be strolling in his grave if he heard you. All his life he was proud of the fact that he never had to rely on debt to keep this farm running. And now…

GREG: All businesses have debt these days. You can't grow without it. You took on debt when you bought new land.

JERRY: I was careful.

GREG: And you think I'm not?

JERRY: I'll tell you this. When you take this farm over /

GREG: When I take it over?

JERRY: When you take this farm over, I don't know what's going to happen to it.

GREG: Just because you're too cheap to spend fifteen hundred dollars on a hundred and twenty-five thousand dollar tractor.

SUSAN and MARLENE enter.

MARLENE: That sounds like enough. Jerry, maybe you could help Susan load up a couple of boxes?

JERRY: Boxes? *(JERRY indicates his broken leg.)*

SUSAN: I can't load them myself. I'm still wearing my good clothes from school.

JERRY: What makes you think Greg doesn't need me out here?

GREG: I'll give Susan a hand. I could use a break.

MARLENE: I bet you could. This job looks like hard work.

GREG: Yeah. A break from the work would be nice too. Come on Susan. Let's go to your room and get those boxes.

SUSAN: You mean that place that used to be my room.

GREG and SUSAN exit, talking together. MARLENE and JERRY pause.

GREG: *(On his way offstage.)* I don't know what Andrea has planned for that room.

SUSAN: *(On her way offstage.)* What was going on out here with you and Dad? And how come you're spending so much money?

MARLENE glares at JERRY until he breaks the silence.

JERRY: Susan's still moving stuff out of here?

MARLENE: Yes. And she's still upset.

JERRY: Because she married a band teacher?

MARLENE: Oh come on Jerry. She grew up on this farm. And she doesn't feel at home in that grungy duplex. She's having a hard time finding her place.

JERRY: Her place is in town with her husband and his chihuahua. She made her bed, there's no use spilling milk in it.

MARLENE: Why were you fighting with Greg?

JERRY: It wasn't a fight. It was a business discussion. About the tractor.

MARLENE: That's not how it sounded.

JERRY: You always think you know what's going on. But you don't.

MARLENE: I'm going back to town. Do you want a ride? Or is Kate Richards picking you up?

JERRY: Very funny. Greg can run me in later. I'm gonna take a look at this damn clutch.

Scene 6

A few days later—Monday, June 20, 2005.

The Wilson farmhouse.

GREG is alone in the house, talking on the phone. There is paper and a laptop computer spread out on the table.

GREG: *(Into the phone.)* Yeah, things are fine out here Andrea. I'm fine. Looking forward to seeing you tonight.

MARLENE enters from outside, without knocking, followed by JERRY. JERRY's leg is healing but he still has the crutches.

JERRY: Don't you think we should knock?

MARLENE: Shhh. He's on the phone.

GREG: *(Still into the phone.)* What? Again?... Good thing we kept the apartment for another month... I know. ... No. I don't want you to give up your job... I'll figure out something for supper. Don't worry... See you tomorrow night... I love you too.

GREG hangs up the phone. JERRY and MARLENE are silent.

There's a conference at her office this week. She has lots to do.

MARLENE: Oh Greg.

JERRY: It doesn't look good around town. People are wondering what's going on out here.

GREG: I wasn't expecting you two out here today.

JERRY: I wanted to pick up the binoculars.

GREG: Why?

JERRY: Something's going on in Roy Bailey's house and I can just about see in from the kitchen window.

GREG: Oh geez.

MARLENE: I was hoping to sneak a little bit of lettuce from the garden, unless you think Andrea would mind.

GREG: Go ahead.

JERRY: Take it easy, Marlene. Remember: other men's squashes are not your squashes.

GREG: I'll warn you—it's not pretty out there. We're behind with the weeding.

JERRY: We could see that from the road.

MARLENE: Don't worry Jerry. I won't pick any weeds.

MARLENE pulls a plastic bag from her pocket and goes outside.

GREG: Did you want to take a look at that new clutch in the tractor?

JERRY: I told the Elks I'd help out at the rec centre. They re-paint the playground equipment every summer.

GREG: It's good to see you getting involved.

JERRY: If I don't help those guys, I don't know what kind of mess they'll make. Especially with that Jeff Murphy hanging around. You can lead an Elk to paint, but you can't make him think… What's this all over the table?

GREG: Just crunching some numbers.

JERRY: What numbers?

GREG: Nothing much. That durum crop across the highway sure is something, hey?

JERRY: Yeah. What about those numbers?

GREG: I think this would be a good year to replace the grain truck.

JERRY: It's always something with you, isn't it? There's nothing wrong with my grain truck. It's in great shape.

GREG: We had to wait two days for new parts when it broke down in the middle of harvest last year. I can't afford to do that again.

JERRY: Now that it's fixed it'll run just /

GREG: Now that it's fixed it's a thirty-year old truck with a few new parts… No use having a great crop if I can't haul it home.

JERRY: But /

GREG: I looked on the internet. I think I found a good one up in North Battleford. I might run up there tomorrow and give it a test drive.

JERRY: Oh, I see.

GREG: Why don't you come along and see it for yourself?

JERRY: Not much point, is there? You've already decided.

GREG: Well I /

JERRY: I've been running this place just fine for decades. But suddenly nothing's good enough. First it's a new clutch in the tractor. Then it's a brand new truck. With a brand new stereo, I suppose.

GREG: You know as well as I do—I have to keep up. Or before you know it, I'll be trying to farm with a rusted-up line of old equipment.

JERRY: Rusted up, is it?

GREG: That's not what I'm saying.

JERRY: You'll get a new grain truck over my dead body. I've been farming longer than you've been alive. If we needed a new grain truck, I'd know it.

GREG: What?

JERRY: You heard me.

GREG: Who's running this place?

JERRY: I thought we were working together.

GREG: You were gonna retire. I was gonna make the decisions.

JERRY: You need to show a little more commitment and get a little more experience before you /

GREG: I'm thirty-five years old. There's plenty of other things I could be doing.

JERRY: Some secret job that comes with three thousand acres of land and a shed full of equipment?

GREG: There are places where I get treated with respect. Where people appreciate my expertise.

JERRY: You think I didn't learn anything running this place for thirty-eight years?

GREG: That's not what I said.

JERRY: You said you think you're smarter than your old man. And you wanta send me to the nursing home to sit on my ass in a rocking chair. Smoking a pipe all day while you run this farm into the ground.

GREG: A pipe? You don't even smoke cigarettes. You're crazy.

JERRY: I doubled the size of this farm. And not so you

could treat it like a roll of quarters in a Las Vegas casino.

GREG: You've lost your mind. I've had enough.

GREG slams his laptop shut.

JERRY: What?

GREG: I've had enough. I'm getting out of here.

JERRY: Where would you go?

GREG: I could slip back into my old life tomorrow morning without missing a beat.

JERRY: Leave the farm?

GREG: There's nothing for me here. You'll never let go.

JERRY: That's not true.

GREG: You said it out loud! I'll get to make a decision about this farm over your dead body.

JERRY: About the grain truck… I was talking about the grain truck…

GREG exits into the rest of the house.

What are you doing?

GREG: *(From offstage.)* Packing.

JERRY: Packing? Why?

GREG: *(From offstage.)* You heard me. I'm leaving.

JERRY: But…

GREG emerges carrying a hastily-packed shaving kit or knapsack. Maybe with a T-shirt or sock hanging out the half-done-up zipper.

GREG: I'm not like you. I make a decision and I stick to it.

I decide to leave and I leave. I don't hang around like a bad smell, driving everybody nuts.

JERRY: But… OK, look. Maybe we could get a new grain truck next year.

GREG: You don't get it, do you?

JERRY: You can't leave. Who's gonna do the farm work?

GREG: Good question.

JERRY: And I can't do all the spraying by myself! I'm on crutches!

GREG: No kidding?

JERRY: And how can anybody take the Wilson farm seriously if we can't figure out who's running the place?

GREG: I won't be here to worry about that, will I?

GREG leaves, slamming the door behind him.

JERRY: But I will.

GREG storms back in, picks his laptop up from the kitchen table, puts it under his arm, and takes it with him as he leaves again.

GREG: I doubt you'll be needing this.

We hear a truck door slam and the sound of GREG speeding away. JERRY sits at the table with his head in his hands. MARLENE enters, with a bag of lettuce, and JERRY sits up, alert again.

MARLENE: What's going on?

JERRY: Whattaya mean?

MARLENE: You know what I mean. Why did Greg tear out of here so fast?

JERRY: One of his friends called… He went to town to get together with the guys.

MARLENE: Why such a rush?

JERRY: Damn kids. Who knows?

MARLENE: And why did he have all that stuff with him?

JERRY: Shit. Who knows? …You might as well get back to town.

MARLENE: Now? Without you?

JERRY: I've got some things to do out here.

MARLENE: How'll you get home?

JERRY: I'll bring that damn grain truck to town. I want to take a good look at it anyway.

MARLENE: OK, fine. See you later.

MARLENE leaves the house. JERRY is left alone, forlorn.

End of Act One.

Act Two

Scene 7

A few days later. afternoon. Wednesday, June 22, 2005.

The Wilson farmhouse.

MARLENE is alone in the house, sitting at the kitchen table, drinking a cup of coffee and reading a newspaper. There is a knock at the door.

MARLENE: Come in.

NORMA opens the door and peeks around it before entering.

NORMA: Oh! Marlene. I wasn't expecting you to be here again.

MARLENE: Hello Norma. This is a great article about the Homecoming weekend in the Stony Valley Review.

NORMA: Yes, it turned out well. They printed it almost exactly the way I sent it in.

MARLENE: What are you up to today?

NORMA: I was just driving by and I thought I'd check in on Andrea again.

MARLENE: Driving by?

NORMA: Cleaning out the garage. Taking a few old things out to the garbage dump.

MARLENE: I see.

NORMA: So, is Andrea here?

MARLENE: She's working in the city today.

NORMA: That's a shame. I'll have to try another day. What are you doing out here?

MARLENE: I'm just tagging along with Jerry. He wanted to use the tools out here to fix my blender.

NORMA: I'm glad I found you out here. There's something I wanted to talk to you about.

MARLENE: What's that?

NORMA: I hate to ask, if you're busy. You don't owe me any favours. Not after that Ladies' Bonspiel.

MARLENE: Oh, please. Forget about that. I have.

NORMA: Have you?

MARLENE: Yes, I was just a sub. And it was too late in the game for my trademark double take-out to save it anyway. But that's behind us.

NORMA: If you say so.

MARLENE: What can I do for you?

NORMA: I thought maybe you'd like to use some of your free time to give me a hand with the Homecoming books.

MARLENE: The books?

NORMA: You know how government grants are. They want so much paperwork, it's hardly worth the money.

MARLENE: I'm not scared of a few forms.

NORMA: I could do it myself. But I've got quite a lot on my plate right now.

MARLENE: Oh. Well, I guess I could help out.

NORMA: Good. We'll be able to celebrate in style.

JERRY enters from outside.

JERRY: Relax Norma, you don't have to celebrate just because I came in.

NORMA: How could we help ourselves, Jerry?

MARLENE: Norma was talking about government grants for the Homecoming celebration.

JERRY: If Calvert wants to revitalize rural Saskatchewan, he might as well give us money to throw a party.

NORMA: It's more than a party. It's a celebration to showcase the community.

JERRY: So we can impress all those hotshots that come home from Alberta with their oil money.

NORMA: Marlene, can you come by later this afternoon? There's only nine days left until the party, and so much to do.

MARLENE: Is three-ish alright?

NORMA: Great. And don't forget about the Committee meeting tonight.

MARLENE: Seven o'clock?

NORMA: That's right. At my place. Will Andrea be there?

JERRY: Greg said she'd likely be working late.

NORMA: She certainly is spending a lot of time in the city.

MARLENE: I'll leave a note for her.

NORMA: Good. And how are you Jerry?

JERRY: Can't complain.

MARLENE: Oh really?

NORMA: Looks like that leg's healing up. Are you exercising?

MARLENE: I keep telling him he should do more stretching. Maybe some yoga.

NORMA: I hear you've been spending quite a bit of time out here. I hope you're giving Greg a chance to make his own decisions.

JERRY: Of course I am. Don't worry about the Wilson farm. Life's a bowl of berries out here. I've got so much free time, maybe I'll buy that fifth wheel that's cluttering up your driveway. Take it out on the open road.

NORMA: Yes. Leonard passed away before we could use it.

MARLENE: This is the first I've heard of you wanting to go anywhere further than the Esso.

JERRY: I went skiing.

NORMA: I'd better get back to town and get ready for the Health Board meeting. Oh, one more thing before I go—do you think Andrea would mind making some pies for the Friday night barbeque?

MARLENE: I don't think she bakes much. And she's so busy. But I could pick some up for you. The new Safeway bakery /

NORMA: No, that's fine. You're already looking after the condiments. I'll find enough. Susan's going to make a few cherry pies.

MARLENE: Really? Susan?

NORMA: She said she found some of Jerry's mother's recipes mixed up with some old books she took to town. She's been practicing.

MARLENE: On her own?

NORMA: I think she might have called Olive Richards for some tips.

MARLENE: I don't know why she'd bother. If you work it all out, it's cheaper to buy them. And she said Scott thought she didn't have time to volunteer right now, at the end of the school year.

NORMA: She must've changed her mind. Or his. Funny she didn't tell you. Did she mention she's taking that vacant spot on the Library Board? That spot I offered you.

MARLENE: Well. Good for her.

NORMA: And don't worry about Andrea bringing pie. There's lots of other farm wives who /

JERRY: No, no! Andrea loves baking. Of course she'll make pie.

MARLENE: Jerry, you can't make commitments for Andrea.

JERRY: Greg's wife loves to pitch in.

NORMA: Great. Can she make five?

JERRY: I'll let her know.

MARLENE: You do that Jerry.

NORMA: And one more thing. Marlene, there's going to be an opening on the Music Festival Committee next year. Are you interested?

MARLENE: I don't know… Who's leaving the Committee?

NORMA: Ron Bailey's wife. She's leaving him, apparently. Moving back to Calgary.

MARLENE: Oh, that's too bad.

NORMA: Young people are like that these days. They can't keep commitments. Just move on to the next thing when the going gets rough.

JERRY: Yeah. Terrible attitude. Don't know how they'll get ahead..

MARLENE: I'll think about it and get back to you Norma.

NORMA: I'd better get on the road.

NORMA crosses to the door, almost leaves, and steps back in.

Jerry, did I see Dave Reimer's truck out by your shop?

JERRY: Yep.

NORMA: What's he doing today?

JERRY: He wanted me to ask Greg to take a look at his lentil crop. He thinks it might have some disease. Why?

NORMA: No reason. Just curious. Anyway, I'll get going.

JERRY: Remember, curiosity fed the cat.

MARLENE: See you later.

NORMA: Three o'clock.

NORMA exits, and we hear her car door open and close

MARLENE: I can't believe you. Telling her you "can't complain." You can't stop complaining.

JERRY: You know how it is with Norma. In one ear and out her mouth.

MARLENE: That's not true. We don't have anything to hide anyway. We're not even interesting.

JERRY: Norma sure is. She's been chasing poor old Dave all over town.

MARLENE: Norma? But she's still not over Leonard.

JERRY: That's not what Dave says.

MARLENE: Never mind Dave. Since when do you sign Andrea up to bake pie?

JERRY: What do you want people to think of her? And Greg?

MARLENE: I'm not having anything to do with this. You can talk to Andrea.

JERRY: This party's going to be one helluva wing-ding. I'm glad I'm not on Norma's committee. Are you sure you're up to it?

MARLENE: I could organize it in my sleep. I've planned the school Christmas dinner for five hundred people every year since 1992.

JERRY: If you say so. Are you ready to get back to town? I told some of the Elks I'd meet them at the schoolyard this afternoon. They're putting a second coat of paint on that playground equipment.

MARLENE: Maybe I could come along and help out.

JERRY: I don't think so. The other guys' wives don't usually come to these things. I don't want the guys thinking I can't cross the street without holding your hand.

MARLENE: OK. OK. But do we have to go right away? I was hoping to see Greg.

JERRY: Who knows when he'll be back? Let's get going.

MARLENE: I'd really like to wait…

JERRY sneaks his cell phone out of his pocket and hits buttons on it without MARLENE seeing. The house phone rings and he slips his cell phone back into his pocket. MARLENE moves to answer the house phone, but JERRY gets to it first.

JERRY: *(Into the phone.)* Hello?… Hi Greg… I thought you were coming right in. Oh? You decided to go to town?… Your mother's here. She was hoping to see you… I'll let her know. See you later, Greg.

That was Greg.

MARLENE: So I gathered.

JERRY: He went to town. For some chemical. He says to tell you hello.

MARLENE: Fine then. We might as well go. Just let me write a note for Andrea.

JERRY: Let's get going. You can leave a message on the answering machine later.

MARLENE: Oh alright.

MARLENE and JERRY exit.

Scene 8

The next day, late morning—Thursday, June 23, 2005.

The Wilson farmhouse.

JERRY enters the farmhouse without knocking. He no longer has his crutches, but he has a cane with him. He occasionally forgets to use it—his leg is healing well. He's wearing work clothes, sweaty and dirty. He brings in a few grocery bags, and a a large plywood cut-out of a person's torso (meant to resemble GREG.). Ideally, it is built so that one wooden arm will wave if you pull a lever or handle. He's brought the cutout into the house so he can dress it in an old shirt. He admires it, making the arm wave. Or perhaps even sits up on the table beside it, demonstrating sitting beside the cut-out in the car, steering, waving, and making the torso's arm wave as if it were someone sitting in the passenger seat.

JERRY: This should do the trick.

JERRY picks up his cutout and exits. A few seconds later, there is a knock at the door, and MARLENE enters.

MARLENE: Hello? Anybody home?

MARLENE looks around the room and sees a hat JERRY has left behind on the table (or maybe his cane.).

Jerry?

MARLENE snoops through the grocery bags on the table, then goes to the kitchen, just as JERRY enters from outside. When MARLENE comes back to the dining room, JERRY surprises her.

Jerry! What are you doing here?

JERRY: I'm helping Greg with the spraying.

MARLENE: When I come out here you say I'm interfering. You've been 'interfering' with the spraying every morning this week.

JERRY: Not every morning, Marlene. It was too windy on Tuesday.

MARLENE: You know what I mean.

JERRY: I'm giving the kid a hand. That's what fathers do.

MARLENE: You never stop by the duplex to help Susan and Scott.

JERRY: The duplex? What am I gonna do at the duplex? Tighten the bolts on Scott's drum set? Give the chihuahua a haircut? Greg's trying to run a three thousand acre farm by himself.

MARLENE: Alright. I see Andrea's been shopping for baking supplies. Is she here?

JERRY: No… She's working in the city today.

MARLENE: I don't think I've seen her for almost a week.

JERRY: That's not true. You were talking to her the day before yesterday.

MARLENE: No I wasn't…

JERRY: Are you sure? Cut the girl a pair of slacks Marlene. It's tough settling into a new job.

MARLENE: Fine. Where's Greg?

JERRY: Still out spraying.

MARLENE: The sprayer's out in the yard.

JERRY: Then he must be in the shop.

MARLENE: Ah. I'll just go out there and say hello.

JERRY: Why don't you stay in here? I just put some coffee on.

MARLENE: You put the coffee on?

JERRY: Sit down. He'll be in any minute. And we've barely spent any time together, since we've moved to town.

MARLENE: Whose fault is that? You're the one who's out here every day. Or flitting around all over town. If it's not the Elks it's the Esso. Or the rec centre.

JERRY: You wanted me to get out more.

MARLENE: I didn't know you'd be out every day of the week.

JERRY: You almost sound like you miss me.

MARLENE: I am spending a lot of time by myself these days.

JERRY: Even when you had that job you never worked in the summer.

MARLENE: Other summers I've had the garden to look after. And this yard. And you were in and out of the house all day.

JERRY: Aren't you supposed to be busy with that Homecoming Committee?

MARLENE: Don't get me started. Do you know what happened at the meeting yesterday?

JERRY: *(Checking his watch.)* What?

MARLENE: Norma let those women spend an hour debating what kind of syrup to buy for the pancake breakfast on Sunday.

JERRY: There's more than one kind of syrup?

MARLENE: I used to order a year's worth of paper supplies for the whole school in less than half an hour. Now I'm part of a sixty minute free-for-all about syrup.

JERRY: You just said you don't have enough to do.

MARLENE glares at JERRY. There is a knock at the door.

Saved by the knock.

MARLENE: Come on in!

NORMA enters.

NORMA: Oh, hello Marlene. Jerry. I just stopped in to see Andrea. About the Homecoming.

JERRY: She's at work.

NORMA: I guess I wasted my trip out here.

JERRY: Nice try Norma. I saw you go by here on your way to the dump again a while ago.

MARLENE: Again?

NORMA: Just a few old things to get rid of.

NORMA pulls a few books of tickets out of her purse and hands it to MARLENE.

Since I'm here…do you think Andrea'd mind selling some raffle tickets for the Drop-In-Centre quilt?

MARLENE: She's still new in the area…and she's so busy /

JERRY: Of course she'll sell tickets.

NORMA: OK. Lots of women are selling two books or more. Susan asked for three.

MARLENE: Three? Did she?

JERRY: Leave three for Andrea then. She'll sell them. No problem.

NORMA: And what about you? I don't suppose you'd want to take a book or two?

MARLENE: Well, why not? I don't have to sell anything for the school, now that I'm retired. I'll take a couple of books.

NORMA hands a handful of ticket books to MARLENE and sets more on the table.

NORMA: I'll leave Andrea's tickets too.

MARLENE: Anything else we can do for you?

NORMA: That's all for right now.

JERRY: I've gotta get out to the shop and help Greg.

NORMA: Nice seeing you, Jerry.

MARLENE: I'm going back to town soon. Can you invite Greg and Andrea for supper tonight? We can eat late, after she gets home from work.

JERRY: Sure. But they might be too busy.

JERRY exits.

MARLENE: I think there's some iced tea in the fridge. Can I get you a glass?

NORMA: I'd like that. As long as Andrea won't mind.

MARLENE: Why would Andrea mind?

NORMA: Having her mother-in-law in her kitchen while she's not home.

MARLENE: Oh… I suppose…

NORMA: Maybe nobody will tell her.

MARLENE: Maybe.

NORMA: You're lucky to have both your kids so close by. I haven't seen Shane and the grandkids since Thanksgiving.

NORMA pulls herself together, looks around the room, and changes the subject.

I haven't been here much in the past few years. Whatever happened to that old macramé hanging you used to have up on this wall?

MARLENE: Old?

NORMA: No offense, Marlene. I have one too. Remember? We made them together at that Regional College class.

MARLENE: We'd do anything to get out of the house back then.

NORMA: That's for sure. Remember when the College put on that haircutting course?

MARLENE: I'd forgotten all about that.

NORMA: I'm sure the kids haven't. I can't believe they let us practice on them... I wonder if I still have the photos.

MARLENE: Susan and Greg ripped mine up and put them in the burning barrel. I wasn't cut out for hairdressing.

NORMA: Neither was I. But what about your wall hanging? I still have mine, you know. It's in my upstairs hallway.

MARLENE: I wasn't sure how it would fit in the new place. So I left it here for Andrea. But I can see why she wouldn't want to leave it up. It doesn't mean anything to her.

NORMA: It must be hard for you, having someone else move into the home you lived in for so long.

MARLENE: Yes, I suppose it is. I hoped I'd be able to handle it gracefully if Andrea wanted to make a lot of changes. At least she hasn't had time to do much in the yard, or the garden.

NORMA: In some ways it's good that Shane never wanted to farm. There was no daughter-in-law moving into my old house.

MARLENE: That must've been such a disappointment for Leonard.

NORMA: It'll be five years next week.

MARLENE: Five years already since Leonard's accident? It seems like just last month.

NORMA: Not for me. The time went so slow. Especially those first couple of years.

MARLENE: Oh Norma. But you've kept so busy since you moved to town.

NORMA: Why do you think I do all those things?

MARLENE: I'm sorry Norma. Leonard was a good man.

NORMA: He was. I miss having someone to talk to. To share things with. You're lucky to still have Jerry.

MARLENE: Oh, trust me. Jerry doesn't share everything.

There is a pause while NORMA pulls herself together and changes the subject.

NORMA: The Homecoming plans are coming along well.

MARLENE: You have lots of help.

NORMA: Too much, sometimes.

MARLENE: I wouldn't have the patience to run those meetings.

NORMA: It's not always easy. Alice Ridgeway wants to make her apple-ham strudel for the barbeque.

MARLENE: Oh dear.

NORMA: And it gets frustrating, waiting for everyone to say their piece about every little decision.

MARLENE: You feel that way too?

NORMA: Sure! Was it any different for you? School staff meetings with all the teachers? Or handling the school board?

MARLENE: No, I guess not.

NORMA: There's a lot of tricks to handling a group of volunteers. People like to talk. I try to lead them get to the right decision.

MARLENE: Hmmm. I'll watch you more carefully at the next meeting.

NORMA: Monday night. Seven o'clock.

MARLENE: I was thinking about that. That'll be only five days before the Homecoming Barbeque. You should… You might want to think about holding the meeting at the Elks Hall instead of your house—so everyone can take a look at the place to make sure it's ready for Friday.

NORMA: That's not a bad idea.

Lights out.

Scene 9

The next day—Friday, June 24, 2005.

The Wilson farmhouse.

JERRY is at the table in the farmhouse. He's making pie. He has a full mixing bowl, a rolling pin, flour dusted on himself, and a recipe book propped up on the kitchen table.

JERRY: 'Let the dough rest before you roll it'.

JERRY has just started to deal with the dough in the mixing bowl when the house phone rings. JERRY dusts off his hands and answers it.

Hello?…

JERRY realizes he's answered GREG's phone, and tries to disguise his voice to sound more like GREG.

Hi Tim. This is Greg… I do not sound like my old man… Really? You saw me in town? I didn't see you, or I would've got Dad to stop… Of course I'm still living out here. Didn't you just see me?… No! My old man—my father—doesn't tell me what to do!… No, I don't have time for a drink tonight. Lots to do… Yep… 'Bye.

JERRY hangs up the phone and talks in his own voice again.

What kind of a jerk do Greg's friends think I am? *(JERRY turns back to his dough and recipe book.)* "Handle the dough as little as possible." What do they think I'm trying to do?… "Roll out top crust, and cut designs into pastry." Designs?… "Trim edges, and flute." Flute?

MARLENE comes to the door. She knocks lightly, then enters without waiting for an answer. JERRY jumps when she enters, and quickly hides the evidence of his baking while steering her to the living room.

Hi. Uh…glad you're here. I think there's…uh… something wrong with the radio. Maybe you can fix it.

MARLENE is distracted and walks toward the radio while JERRY finishes cleaning up.

MARLENE: What makes you think I could fix a radio?

JERRY: You're always saying women can do anything. What're you doing, anyway, coming in here without knocking?

MARLENE: I knocked.

JERRY: You don't just knock. You wait for someone to answer. No point knocking if you're not going to wait for an answer.

MARLENE: What's the matter with you?

JERRY: You don't live here. You have to knock, you know.

MARLENE: Look who's talking.

JERRY: That's different. This is a farm. Men are supposed to help on farms.

MARLENE: What are women supposed to do? Curl up on the couch and wait to die?

JERRY: Nobody said that, Marlene. But Greg and Andrea might like a little more privacy.

MARLENE looks around the room.

MARLENE: Andrea's really left a mess.

JERRY: No kidding. Can you believe she took off for the city with the place looking like this?

MARLENE: Looks like she's in the middle of baking.

JERRY: She's flighty.

MARLENE: So where's Greg?

JERRY: Greg's...taken his truck to town to get it looked at.

MARLENE: But wasn't he just in town? With you?

JERRY: What?

MARLENE: Alec said he'd seen you and Greg driving around town. Said he tried to flag you down.

JERRY: Guess I didn't see him.

MARLENE: And Eileen said she saw you drive by the post office. The two of you waving like lunatics.

JERRY: There's too darn many windows in that post office... We went to town to see if the guys at the dealership could look at Greg's truck.

MARLENE: So you dropped his truck off?

JERRY: We came back here and then he took it in.

MARLENE: After all those years of giving me a bad time about making extra trips to town. Why are you out here anyway?

JERRY: I'm changing the oil in the lawn tractor. Just came in to go to the bathroom. And have a glass of water.

MARLENE: That's a good idea. I'll get one too.

MARLENE heads for the kitchen, JERRY blocks her.

JERRY: I'll get you some. Sit down and relax. You spend enough time in the kitchen.

MARLENE: *(Sitting down.)* Retirement is certainly changing you.

JERRY goes to the kitchen while she talks to him. There is a knock at the door. MARLENE goes to answer it, but SUSAN enters before MARLENE can get there. SUSAN's carrying a gardening magazine.

(Loudly, so JERRY can hear.) Susan! Give Greg and Andrea a chance to answer the door before you come in. You don't live here anymore.

JERRY: *(From the kitchen.)* Oh for crying out loud.

SUSAN: Sorry Mom. I forgot again.

JERRY comes back with a glass of water for MARLENE.

SUSAN: I came out to see if Andrea was here. I thought maybe she could use some help in the garden.

MARLENE: Andrea's not home.

JERRY: Greg and Andrea have everything under control.

MARLENE: You weren't that interested in helping in the garden when I lived here.

SUSAN: You never needed my help. And I was just reading an article about a good way to tie up cabbage plants. Since there's no garden at the duplex, I thought it would be a good way for me to spend some time with Andrea.

MARLENE: Oh. I'm sure Andrea would have liked that.

SUSAN: When will she be home?

MARLENE: Well, I think she /

JERRY: She's in the city. Who knows when she'll get back?

SUSAN: Wow. She sure left this place a mess.

JERRY: Give the woman a break, would you? I don't know why the two of you are so mean.

SUSAN: Mean? I came out here to help.

MARLENE: Really Jerry. That's enough. Susan, I'm on my way back to town. You don't want to come and have a coffee with me in the new house, do you?

SUSAN: I need to pick up Scott from the jazz band rehearsal. They're going to play at the Homecoming barbeque.

JERRY: I can't wait.

MARLENE: *(To SUSAN.)* Really?

SUSAN: Yes. I was talking about Norma about it at the Library Board meeting.

MARLENE: Oh, I see.

SUSAN: There sure are a lot of things going on in town.

SUSAN exits.

MARLENE: I'd better get going too, Jerry.

There's a pause. MARLENE sighs, turns to leave, then comes back.

I almost forgot. The phone in town's been ringing

off the hook for you. I don't know why those guys can't use your cell phone.

JERRY: Who's calling?

MARLENE: Alec called about the Elks elections again. They want you to be the President, or the Grand Poobah, or whatever they call it.

JERRY: Exalted Ruler. Me? Huh. That'd be something.

MARLENE: And Rick called. He's got an empty spot on his annual Guys Only Fishing Trip.

JERRY: Oh? He used to invite me on that trip all the time.

MARLENE: You've got more time this year. Greg can manage without you for a few days in mid-July.

JERRY: Yeah. Well. We'll see.

MARLENE: I'm going to head back to town. Why don't you come with me?

JERRY: You go ahead. I've got a couple of things to finish up out in the shop.

MARLENE: Alright. Unless your arm's too sore from all that waving.

JERRY: Huh?

MARLENE: Never mind. I guess I'll find something to do in town.

JERRY: It's your own fault if you're sitting home alone. I'm finding lots to do.

MARLENE: Yes. You are. Jerry, there isn't anything you want to tell me, is there?

JERRY: You don't think I'm driving off to the city to take some kind of exercise class? I wouldn't be caught dead in a condominium. I'm busy, that's all.

MARLENE: Alright. Alright. I'm going "home".

MARLENE exits.

Scene 10

Tuesday, June 28, 2005.

The Wilson farmhouse.

We hear machinery (a sprayer) driving into the yard. MARLENE opens the entrance into the farmhouse from outside and steps halfway in. Then we hear squealing tires. MARLENE turns to look outside, then stands half in the door, talking towards the outside.

NORMA: *(Offstage.)* Roy! Roy! Are you OK?

MARLENE: That was close!

NORMA: *(Offstage.)* Oh Roy. What a scare. You go home and take it easy for a while.

MARLENE: Roy, I'm so sorry.

MARLENE and NORMA enter. We hear a car drive away.

My goodness. That could have been awful. I'm so sorry, Norma.

NORMA: Roy's OK. It could've been worse.

JERRY enters.

MARLENE: Jerry Wilson, what was that?

JERRY: What?

MARLENE: Don't give me "what". You almost hit Roy with your sprayer.

JERRY: Oh, that. Time and herbicide wait for no man. I was in a hurry to get home so I can get to the summerfallowing. That stringbean Roy's all skin and bones anyway. Don't think a little machinery could hurt him. Why was he prowling around our yard anyway?

NORMA: I brought him out to do some taping.

JERRY: Taping?

NORMA: Marlene managed to get the last minute paperwork done. Thanks to her, we got the video grant.

JERRY: What's that? Government money for a new VCR?

NORMA: It's a 2005 Centennial grant. They're giving out money so communities can record their town celebrations.

JERRY: Movies of a bunch of dopes standing around the Elks Hall?

NORMA: I'm sure everyone in town will want a copy. And they'll put the best ones on the internet.

JERRY: Oh boy.

NORMA: Roy's so excited. He's been doing all the audio-visual work at the school since he was in eighth grade.

JERRY: But why's he filming here?

MARLENE: The Elks Hall isn't the best place for the Friday night barbeque.

NORMA: I know it's last minute… With the barbeque in just four days. It's a good thing Marlene thought of holding the last meeting at the Elks Hall. I'd forgotten.

JERRY: What's wrong with the Elks Hall?

MARLENE: It's so stuffy in there. If there's a crowd and it gets hot…

NORMA: And the Elks don't always…think of maintenance as a priority.

JERRY: That Jeff Murphy.

MARLENE: So the Elks Hall isn't the best place for a big celebration like this. Not with so many people from out of town here.

NORMA: Marlene—I can't believe I forgot to tell you! I had a letter this morning—the Lieutenant Governor's coming for the Friday night barbeque.

MARLENE: What? Lynda Haverstock's coming to Stony Valley? That's fantastic. I just love her.

NORMA: She sure has a lot of class.

JERRY: If you don't want to use the Elks Hall, why not have the Barbeque out behind the rec centre?

NORMA: The 4-H Club is having a demonstration there on Friday morning.

JERRY: So?

NORMA: There'll be a lot of…horses.

MARLENE: We can't have Lynda Haverstock traipsing though a bunch of horse manure.

JERRY: It won't be anything new. Don't forget she was the leader of the Saskatchewan Liberals.

MARLENE: Jerry!

NORMA: We don't want visitors to get a bad impression.

JERRY: Darn oil guys coming back from Alberta like they're better than us… So where are you having the barbeque?

MARLENE: Here.

JERRY: What?

MARLENE: Here on the farm. Agriculture's the heart of Stony Valley.

NORMA: And you've both worked so hard to keep this place looking good all these years.

JERRY: You're forgetting something, Marlene.

MARLENE: What's that?

JERRY: This isn't our place anymore. We can't go renting it out like a motel room. You need to ask Greg and Andrea.

NORMA: Where are they?

JERRY: They're not here, are they? So you'll have to hold the barbeque somewhere else.

MARLENE: Where are they?

JERRY: Andrea's working in the city. And Greg's…Greg's gone to the city too.

NORMA: The ladies in town really haven't seen much of Andrea. They're starting to wonder.

MARLENE: They sure are.

NORMA: Alice Ridgeway was asking if Andrea might've married Greg just so she could divorce him and take half the farm.

JERRY: Why would they say that?

MARLENE: Don't worry Jerry. When I told them Andrea would love to host the barbeque, they realized she's serious about being part of this place for the long run.

JERRY: Oh. Heck. You're right Norma, there's no point

waiting around. I'm sure the kids'll have the barbeque out here.

NORMA: Oh, no, you were right. I'll talk to them before we finalize anything.

JERRY: I'll settle this. I'll just call Greg's cell.

JERRY dials the phone and waits for a minute.

Hi Greg. Your dad here… Your mother and I were just wondering if it would be OK to have the Stony Valley Homecoming Barbeque out here at the farm on Friday night. The Elks Hall isn't working out… Yeah? You don't mind?

NORMA: Make sure he knows there'll be more than five hundred people!

MARLENE: Let me talk to him.

JERRY: Yep… Norma says to tell you there'll be lots of people here… Alright, great. Fine. See you when you get home… Yep… Oh, and your mom says hi… Bye.

JERRY hangs up the phone.

He says having the barbeque here is OK with him.

MARLENE: Jerry, I wanted to talk to him.

JERRY: The kid doesn't want to talk to his mommy while he's in the middle of the Home Depot.

MARLENE: Shouldn't you check with Andrea?

JERRY: A guy doesn't need a signed note from his wife for every little thing.

NORMA: Great. That's settled. I'll run back to town. I'm getting my oil changed.

JERRY: I thought they quit doing that at the Esso.

NORMA: Not the Esso. Dave's going to do it.

JERRY: Dave Reimer?

NORMA: Well, he knows how. And he has time.

MARLENE: Oh?

NORMA: Just a little favour. Dave and my Leonard were friends, you know… So I'd better get going.

MARLENE: We'll see you later, Norma.

NORMA: 'Bye.

NORMA exits.

MARLENE: I'm just going to see if there's any iced tea. Do you want any?

JERRY: No thanks.

MARLENE goes to the kitchen. While she's in there, SUSAN enters without knocking. She looks around and sees JERRY.

SUSAN: Oops. Sorry.

JERRY: What?

SUSAN: I don't want another two-hour lecture about knocking.

MARLENE comes out with a glass in her hand.

MARLENE: I see Andrea's made her pies. They look… OK.

JERRY: Just "OK"? They look great.

SUSAN: Good. I thought she might call me to give her a hand, but I didn't hear from her. Nobody in this family ever calls me back. She's sure fitting in around here.

SUSAN goes into the kitchen and comes back right away.

MARLENE: I'm not sure I'd say "great". Why do you care so much?

SUSAN starts talking on her way back from the kitchen.

SUSAN: Wow. I thought my first pies were bad. But it looks like she made these in the dark.

JERRY: Andrea went to a lot of trouble to make those pies. I don't need you two bad-mouthing her.

SUSAN: Give me a break. I've tried to be nice to Andrea. I came out to help with the garden, offered to help her with the pie, phoned her to get together. But she doesn't even return my calls. I thought it would be nice to have a sister-in-law nearby, but I'm having more luck with Norma Janson.

MARLENE: Just give Andrea a bit more time. And maybe the pies taste better than they look.

SUSAN: They'd have to.

JERRY: There's nothing wrong with these pies.

MARLENE: OK, OK. Relax.

SUSAN: Other people have made pies for the Barbeque too.

MARLENE runs her hand over some dust on something near her chair and holds up her finger.

MARLENE: It's sure dusty in here. Look at this.

SUSAN: Even the duplex is cleaner than this.

MARLENE: I hope Andrea gets the house in order before Friday. For the Barbeque.

JERRY: The house? Everyone'll be outside. Or in the shop if it rains.

MARLENE: People will still need to come into the house. We'll need the fridge and the kitchen for the food.

SUSAN: And where do you think people are going to go to the bathroom?

MARLENE: You can't expect Lynda Haverstock to squat out behind the tractor!

SUSAN: What? Lynda Haverstock's coming to Stony Valley? I love her.

JERRY: Oh geez.

MARLENE: Didn't you know that?

SUSAN: Nobody tells me anything.

MARLENE: *(To JERRY.)* And you'd better make sure Greg hauls some water. He'll want a full cistern before this Barbeque.

JERRY: Oh geez.

MARLENE: The kids have so much to do out here. But like you keep reminding me. It's not our place anymore.

SUSAN: Well…anyway…I have news.

JERRY: What kind of news?

MARLENE: News? Oh! Susan! That's wonderful.

SUSAN: Calm down. Not that kind of news.

JERRY: What, then?

SUSAN: We're buying a house!

MARLENE: Really?

SUSAN: Yes! That one down the back alley from yours. Where Ron Bailey was living.

MARLENE: That's great!

JERRY: Humph. Good. I never did like that duplex.

SUSAN: I know. I didn't either. The new place has a great yard. And a brand new kitchen.

MARLENE: Scott said he wasn't ready to buy a house.

SUSAN: I talked him into it. He still thinks the stock market's a better place to save money. But I don't care. I want my own home.

MARLENE: That's great news.

SUSAN: I'm going to go home and start packing. And Mom, could you lend me Grandma's green salad bowl?

MARLENE: That big old glass bowl?

SUSAN: Yes. I know it's not Christmas, but I was thinking of making her jello salad for the Sunday potluck.

MARLENE: Hmmm…

SUSAN: Aunt Jean's coming home from Thunder Bay for the Homecoming, and that's always been her favorite.

MARLNE: The green salad bowl…

SUSAN: I'll be careful with it. I'll bring it back right away on Monday.

MARLENE: It's not that. I'm just not sure exactly which box it's in…

SUSAN: You haven't unpacked it yet? It's a family heirloom.

MARLENE: Well, I haven't needed it… Don't get upset. I'll look for it.

SUSAN: OK. Thanks.

JERRY: Tell the band teacher I'm glad he's taking my lead.

MARLENE: Congratulations.

SUSAN: And Dad, you'd better get rid of those binoculars before we move in.

SUSAN leaves.

MARLENE: I guess I'll get going too. God knows how long it's going to take me to find that damn bowl. I'll see you in town Jerry. You'll need a shower before you go to work with the Elks. I can smell the chemical on you from here... Boy... Andrea's got a lot to do around here before Friday.

MARLENE leaves.

JERRY: *(Sniffing himself.)* Damn Lorsban.

JERRY's cell phone rings. He pulls it from his pocket and looks at the display.

Jeff Murphy.

JERRY opens the phone and answers the call.

Hello?... Oh, hi Jeff... The Oddfellows? Yeah, I said I'd join that... Wednesday night? You mean tomorrow? Yeah, OK. I'll see you at the meeting. Look, I gotta go.

JERRY hangs up his phone and checks his watch.

Damn!

JERRY looks around for the nearest cloth, or maybe his shirt sleeve, and frantically starts dusting.

Scene 11

Thursday, June 30, one day before the barbeque.

The Wilson farmhouse.

There is a pink housecoat hanging on a chair by the door of the house. JERRY is in the house alone.

JERRY: *(To himself.)* I can't believe this…

JERRY hesitates and stalls before making the call, then picks up the phone and dials. When the answering machine picks up at the other end, he speaks into the phone.

Greg? It's your dad again. Look. I know I've been a jerk. You know more about farming than I've been giving you credit for. It's your turn to take a shot at things out here… Look, I already left a bunch of messages about the big Homecoming barbeque we're having out here tomorrow night. If you don't come I…I don't know what I'll tell everybody… Please.

JERRY hangs up the phone, then shakes his head and rolls his eyes, unable to believe what he's done. MARLENE knocks on the door and enters, carrying a bag. NORMA is following right behind.

NORMA: Hello Jerry, out here again, are you?

JERRY: Marlene—I didn't know you were coming out here.

MARLENE: You were already gone when I woke up. I ran into Norma in the yard, looking for Andrea.

NORMA: I thought I'd drop in and make sure everything's all set for tomorrow.

JERRY: Andrea's not here. But everything's fine for the barbeque.

NORMA: Andrea's here.

MARLENE: Here? Jerry, you said she spent the night in the city.

NORMA: She's here. I saw her from the road about ten minutes ago. On my way to the dump. She waved at me. She was out working in the garden. Wearing this bathrobe. *(She points to the robe hanging on the chair.)*

MARLENE: Outside in her bathrobe? Where is she now Jerry?

JERRY: She, uh, she's…in the shower.

NORMA: Oh good. I'll wait.

JERRY: She might be quite a while.

NORMA: I have time.

JERRY: Humph. I'll leave you women in here to gossip.

NORMA: Dave Reimer says you've been down at the Esso selling tickets on that Drop-In-Centre quilt.

MARLENE: You're selling my tickets?

JERRY: Uh, yeah.

JERRY leaves.

NORMA: That was strange.

MARLENE: Jerry can be a strange man sometimes. You didn't explain why you're out and about so early.

NORMA: Well… Mornings are hard for me. I'm always up looking for something to do, and it's too early to call anyone, or do anything around town.

MARLENE: Oh Norma.

NORMA: I keep hoping it'll get easier.

MARLENE: I thought you had everything together. Everyone was so impressed when you had Leonard's things boxed up and gone before his relatives went back to Yorkton after the funeral.

NORMA: It's not as easy as you think to get rid of someone's things.

MARLENE: If it was Jerry… I don't know how I'd do it.

NORMA: You'd be fine. Your kids are both here. But it has been hard. And…

MARLENE: And what?

NORMA: Oh Marlene… Can I still trust you?

MARLENE: Of course.

NORMA: But you can't say anything to anyone. Not even Jerry.

MARLENE: Jerry and I don't tell each other everything.

NORMA: Oh Marlene. I've been making so many trips to the dump this summer, people are starting to notice.

MARLENE: Jerry was wondering if there was something going on between you and the guy that looks after the dump.

NORMA looks away.

Norma!

NORMA: Elwood doesn't just look after the dump. He runs the grader too. In the winter. And you can tell Jerry there's nothing going on. Elwood just talks to me sometimes.

MARLENE: Oh?

NORMA: And he sometimes lets me into the dump without paying the four-fifty charge.

MARLENE: You're…interested in Elwood?

NORMA: No no no. It's just…

MARLENE: But why do you keep going out to the dump?

NORMA: I got all Leonard's things boxed up right after the funeral, but…

MARLENE: You still have the boxes?

NORMA: No. I've had them in the spare room. Then this spring I thought... I decided it was finally time to move on. So back in March, I took all the boxes out to my car.

MARLENE: You've had Leonard's clothes in the trunk of your car since March?

NORMA: Well, yes.

MARLENE: All this time? Oh, Norma.

NORMA: At first, I just couldn't bring myself to leave his things out there. With all the garbage. And the rats. What if someone poking around the dump recognized his things?

MARLENE: Oh, Norma.

NORMA: And then, when Elwood started talking to me every time I went out there...and with Leonard's things right in the car with me...I felt like I was betraying my husband.

MARLENE: Oh, Norma.

NORMA: So I just keep the boxes in the trunk. Then, the other day, when Dave Reimer was changing my oil I was terrified he'd notice them in there and figure out what was in them.

MARLENE: Oh no. He didn't, did he?

NORMA: No. But it's time for me to finish this. I think I'm finally ready to move on.

MARLENE: With Elwood?

NORMA: No! Not Elwood! ...I'll take one step at a time. It's not going to be easy.

MARLENE: No.

NORMA: And what if I find someone I really am...interested

in? Nobody but Leonard's seen me undressed since 1976! It's been thirty years since someone saw me naked for the first time. And even then, we had the lights out.

MARLENE: But Norma, you look great.

NORMA: And I don't even know what goes where.

MARLENE: What?

NORMA: TVs have changed. Cars have changed. Computers are all new. What if people are doing…"sex"… some whole new way now?

MARLENE: Jerry and I certainly aren't.

NORMA: And with the internet out there… Men might have all kinds of new ideas.

MARLENE: Oh, Norma.

NORMA: But you'll help me? With Leonard's things, I mean.

MARLENE: Of course I will. Don't even worry about the dump. We'll burn the boxes out back. In Greg's burning barrel. Just like that time I found my old school report cards in the basement and I didn't want the kids to see them.

NORMA: Or when I found Leonard's dirty magazines under Shane's bed. Thank you Marlene.

Scene 12

Immediately following.

Jerry's shop.

JERRY is in the shop, cleaning things up, trying to relax.

MARLENE: Jerry? You in here?

MARLENE enters.

JERRY: Yes.

MARLENE: Oh, good. I'm on my way back to town.

JERRY: You're what?

MARLENE: I've got a few things to do.

JERRY: You're not… Did Andrea get out of the shower?

MARLENE: You know how those city women are with their showers. They have no idea about hauling water.

JERRY: Oh, yeah.

MARLENE: Norma and I have other things to do this morning. We'll catch up with Andrea later.

JERRY: Later. Great.

MARLENE: So I guess I'll go back to town.

JERRY: OK. Sounds good.

MARLENE goes to leave, but turns when JERRY calls her back.

Marlene?

MARLENE: Yes?

JERRY: Things have been a little…rushed for me lately.

MARLENE: Yes.

JERRY: Passing the farm on has been harder than I thought.

MARLENE: Yes.

JERRY: I used to watch Dave. Out at his farm. Bothering his son. Meddling. I told myself I'd never be like that.

MARLENE: Greg will be fine.

JERRY: Not if I don't give him a chance to do anything.

MARLENE: I'm glad you realize that.

JERRY: This change hasn't been easy for you, either.

MARLENE: I didn't think you were paying attention.

JERRY: I'm not a complete ass... Things'll be different once we get this damn party out of the way. And the spraying over with.

MARLENE: Then it'll be almost time to start harvest.

JERRY: Yeah. But by then...

MARLENE: Yes?

JERRY: You better get back to town.

MARLENE: I could help you out here. We could spend some time together now.

JERRY: Look, we had a nice little moment here, but I'm busy. I don't have time to stand around brewing the fat all day.

MARLENE: Alright then. Fine. I'll just go. When Andrea gets out of the shower, tell her I've left her a bag of cleaning supplies for the house. So it looks presentable for tomorrow.

MARLENE leaves. JERRY puts his head in his hands.

JERRY: Tomorrow.

Scene 13

Friday July 1, 2005—day of the Homecoming.

The Wilson farmhouse.

The house is scattered with dishes and trays.

MARLENE enters from outside, carrying an empty platter and runs between the kitchen and the dining room, carrying stacks of plates, pies, and cutlery back and forth. NORMA enters without knocking, carrying the big coffee urn.

NORMA: This thing sure needs a good rinse-out. I don't think anyone's used it since the Ridgeway family reunion. And I don't think Alice cleaned it properly after that. She really is starting to lose it.

MARLENE: She set her ham strudel out with the desserts.

NORMA: There's so many people out there!

MARLENE: Yes, it's a great turnout.

JERRY enters.

Oh, there you are Jerry.

NORMA: Jerry, are Andrea and Greg around? I haven't seen them yet this afternoon.

JERRY: They're out in the yard. Behind the shop, I think, introducing those ladies from the nursing home to Lynda Haverstock.

NORMA: Roy's been looking for them. He wants to get them into the video.

JERRY: He'll find them. The yard's not that big.

SUSAN enters.

SUSAN: Are there any plastic cups? I don't know what the Elks were thinking—bringing a keg out here without cups.

JERRY: They put that Jeff Murphy in charge of the bar.

NORMA: Your mother bought all kinds of glasses…

MARLENE or NORMA finds a stack of Styrofoam cups and hands them to SUSAN.

SUSAN: Thanks. And we could put some more pie out too. You won't believe it. People are actually eating Andrea's pie. They must want to make her feel good because she's new in town. Uh oh. I hope she didn't hear that.

MARLENE: Who?

SUSAN: Andrea.

MARLENE: Don't worry. She's not in here.

SUSAN: I heard Dad telling somebody that Andrea came in here to lie down.

NORMA: In the middle of the party? Jerry, why would she do that?

JERRY: She…uh…wasn't feeling well.

NORMA: I hope there's nothing wrong.

JERRY: Just a little stomach ache. Nothing to worry about.

NORMA: Roy really wants to get her on tape. *(NORMA heads toward the exit to the bedrooms.)* I'll just check on her, shall I?

JERRY: *(Grabbing NORMA by the arm and ushering her toward the exit to outside.)* No, no. We wouldn't want to wake her up!

MARLENE: While you're out there, can you check on the salad table?

NORMA: Sure, Marlene.

SUSAN: And can you take these cups out to the Elks?

NORMA: Sure, Susan.

NORMA leaves, with the cups.

SUSAN: If there's something wrong with Andrea, maybe somebody should go in and check on her?

JERRY: She's fine. This is her house. She can go and lie down if she wants to.

SUSAN: I'm just trying to be nice. You don't have to jump all over me.

There is a knock and a voice from offstage.

ROY: *(Offstage.)* Mrs. Wilson? Are you in there? Have you seen Andrea? I really need to get her in the video.

JERRY: The girl's sick, Roy. Come in here and you'll regret it!

ROY: *(Offstage.)* OK! OK!

JERRY: Sheesh. That's the last thing I need in here. Stringbean Roy.

NORMA enters from outside, still talking over her shoulder and carrying the cups.

NORMA: Roy! Go and get some footage of Lynda Haverstock. She's going to sing with the jazz band.

ROY: *(Offstage.)* OK.

NORMA: Marlene, I completely forgot that I meant to take a couple more pies with me.

MARLENE: Oh, no problem. There's lots.

SUSAN: Maybe we could put another one of my pies out.

NORMA: I'll nip in and check on Andrea.

JERRY: No need. She's fine.

MARLENE: Jerry, are you sure? Do you want me to take a quick look?

JERRY moves MARLENE out of the way.

JERRY: I'll check on her.

JERRY exits to the bedrooms.

JERRY: *(Offstage.)* She's fine, Norma.

NORMA: Well, I'd really like to just say hi. *(To ANDREA, in the other room.)* Andrea? Dear? You're not asleep in there are you?

JERRY: *(Offstage, in a falsetto.)* I'm just fine Norma, don't worry about me.

NORMA: You don't sound fine.

JERRY: *(Offstage, in a falsetto.)* Just a sore throat.

NORMA: I thought it was a stomach ache.

JERRY: *(Offstage, in a falsetto.)* You know how these things spread.

NORMA: Spread!... I'm coming in there.

JERRY: *(Offstage, in a falsetto.)* You get back to the guests, Norma! Don't let me ruin the party for you. I know how hard you've worked.

NORMA shoves by MARLENE to exit into the bedrooms.

NORMA: *(Offstage.)* Andrea, it's dark in here! Let me turn on a light and get a look at you.

JERRY: *(Offstage, in a falsetto.)* No, no. My eyes are sore.

MARLENE: Your eyes too?

SUSAN: This doesn't seem right. Doctor Banman's outside. And I don't think he's had too much to drink yet.

NORMA: *(Offstage.)* Let me see for myself.

JERRY: *(From offstage, in a falsetto.)* I'm fine. I just need to rest.

SUSAN: I'm going to find Doctor Banman.

SUSAN heads for the door.

MARLENE: Come back here Susan. I'm sure she's fine.

JERRY enters, dressed in a housecoat with a scarf over his head and thick white cream spread all over his face.

JERRY: *(In a falsetto.)* See? I'm just fine. *(Then, without the falsetto, looking down at himself and realizing how silly he looks.)* Oh geez.

NORMA: Oh Jerry!

MARLENE: This is too far, even for you.

JERRY: Oh geez.

GREG enters from outside. He stands quietly near the door; the others don't see him. He locks the door and pulls the curtains shut so nobody can see inside. He accidentally misses a corner.

SUSAN: Dad? What are you doing? What's going on?

NORMA starts laughing. MARLENE joins her.

MARLENE: Oh Jerry! You didn't think this could work, did you?

SUSAN: I don't get it. Where's Andrea?

JERRY: Andrea's not here.

SUSAN: I can see that. Where is she?

JERRY: You two can quit laughing. This is not funny. Andrea's gone.

SUSAN: Gone? Since when?

JERRY: She's been gone for a week and a half.

SUSAN: So you're wearing women's clothing and giving yourself a facial?

MARLENE: Oh Jerry. I'm sorry.

JERRY: Sorry about what?

MARLENE: I know I shouldn't have…

SUSAN: What?

MARLENE: I wanted to give you some time to calm down and think about things. But then it got carried away.

JERRY: What? You knew?… You knew?

MARLENE: Yes.

JERRY: You knew they left?

MARLENE: Yes.

JERRY looks at NORMA.

JERRY: Did anyone else know?

NORMA: Everyone in town knows.

JERRY: What?

SUSAN: I don't believe this!

MARLENE: Really Jerry. Driving around town with that home-made mannequin? Impersonating Greg on the phone?

NORMA: Standing by the highway in a pink bathrobe.

SUSAN: Why didn't anyone tell me?

NORMA: How did you miss it?

SUSAN: Nobody in this family tells me anything. I don't get it Dad. What does it matter if Andrea's not here?

JERRY: Not just Andrea. Greg.

SUSAN: Greg left too? Why would he do that?

MARLENE: Yes. Why, Jerry?

JERRY: Because I'm an idiot. I couldn't give up control and let Greg take over. And I didn't want anyone to know.

NORMA: This was a great way to keep things quiet.

JERRY: I'm a stubborn old man who couldn't make a change.

NORMA: *(Indicating JERRY's outfit.)* Looks like you've licked that problem.

JERRY: What else was I going to do? Have everyone in town know what an ass I am?

GREG: You're not an ass.

They notice GREG for the first time. JERRY jumps in surprise.

JERRY: Greg? You're back?

GREG: Unless I'm in an episode of *The Twilight Zone*.

JERRY: I didn't want people to find out you'd gone…

GREG: It's not a crime to take a vacation, Dad. Lots of people do it. Mom said it was fine with you.

JERRY: A vacation?

GREG: Yeah. Andrea and I went out to Banff. Camping.

JERRY: But the way you took off outta here… After what we said…

GREG: Yeah. I got as far as your place in town. Mom cooled me down.

MARLENE: I convinced him to take a little holiday. To give you and Greg a chance to think about the farm. Get things in perspective.

JERRY: Why didn't you answer my calls?

GREG: Sorry. We didn't have any cell coverage out in the mountains. I was going to call when we hit Calgary this morning, but my battery was dead.

JERRY: You planned to come home all along?

GREG: You didn't think I'd really abandon the place, did you?

JERRY: What else could I think?

GREG: Mom didn't tell you?

JERRY: No.

GREG: She didn't tell me anything either. I didn't expect to see the yard filled with parked cars and drunken Elks. They're drinking beer right out of the keg out there.

SUSAN looks at the stack of cups.

SUSAN: Oops.

MARLENE: I…didn't think you'd mind.

GREG: What were you doing?

MARLENE: I'll clean up. Don't worry.

GREG: Not the barbeque. Dad. He must've been out of his mind. What must everybody in town think of us. Don't you even care?

JERRY: Wait.

GREG: What?

JERRY: Well… I guess thinking you might be gone for good gave me a chance to see…

GREG: See what?

JERRY: See that I'm glad you're here.

GREG looks at JERRY, surprised.

GREG: If you say so.

SUSAN: Wait a minute. If Andrea's been camping… Who made those pies?

MARLENE: I'm sorry Jerry.

SUSAN: Dad! Not you?… That's a relief. I hoped Andrea could do better than that.

MARLENE: I shouldn't have done this. But it's turning out alright.

ROY: *(Offstage.)* No kidding! This tape is fantastic!

GREG: That sounds like Roy. Is he taping something?

JERRY: Oh shit.

ROY: *(Offstage.)* This is going to be the best tape in the province. This could be my big break.

JERRY: Oh geez.

GREG: Oh boy. Andrea was happy to get home, but I don't know what she's going to make of this.

GREG exits to outside.

ROY: *(Offstage.)* Greg! I've been waiting to get you into the video! Can you come and stand with Andrea and Lynda Haverstock?

GREG: *(Offstage.)* Yeah, alright Roy. If I have to.

NORMA: I'd better go and make sure Lynda's having a good time.

JERRY: You keep this to yourself Norma. People are having enough fun laughing at me. They don't need to think I'm some kind of crass-dressing transvestor.

NORMA: Oh, never mind. Roy's got it all on tape anyway.

NORMA exits.

SUSAN: No wonder Andrea wasn't returning my calls. I'm going to go out and make sure Buffy's coping with this crowd. And I don't know what Scott'll think of all this.

JERRY: Don't you go telling that band teacher anything he doesn't need to know.

SUSAN: I hope this doesn't get me kicked off the Library Board.

SUSAN exits.

MARLENE: Well. Who says that after thirty-seven years of marriage, there's no more surprises.

JERRY: Hmph.

MARLENE: What kind of facial are you giving yourself, anyway?

JERRY: I don't know. But it sure stings.

MARLENE sniffs JERRY's face.

MARLENE: That's Andrea's hair removal cream!

JERRY takes off the housecoat and uses a tea towel to wipe the worst of the cream off his face. He still looks quite ridiculous.

JERRY: I'd better go clean up. Not that it'll make much difference…once everyone's seen the video.

JERRY exits to the bathroom.

Scene 14

A few hours later.

The Wilson farmhouse.

MARLENE and JERRY are in the living room. Sitting down, exhausted.

MARLENE: That was a long day.

JERRY: I can't believe somebody gave Jeff Murphy a license to set off fireworks. Darn government. Good thing I had the cistern full of water to put out that grass fire.

MARLENE: And those oil guys home from Alberta with fire extinguishers in their trucks... Other than that, the party went well. You sure had the place looking good.

JERRY: I can't believe you left me to get things ready all by myself.

MARLENE: I would've helped. If you hadn't been so stubborn. I guess we should get home.

JERRY: I wanta tell you something first.

MARLENE: What?

JERRY: I talked /

There is a knock at the door and NORMA enters.

NORMA: Congratulations you two. That was a great party.

MARLENE: You did the planning.

NORMA: I had a lot of help. A whole committee-full.

MARLENE: Norma, before I forget—I've decided to take that empty spot on the Music Festival Board after all.

NORMA: Good.

MARLENE: And Greg and Andrea say we can use the burning barrel on Tuesday morning.

NORMA: Good. Do you two mind if I leave my car here tonight? There's an Elk passed out in my backseat, and I don't have the heart to wake him up.

MARLENE: Sure. Do you need a lift to town?

NORMA: No. That's OK. Dave's going to drop me off at my place.

Pause.

Well, he's going to town anyway.

MARLENE: You can tell me all about it tomorrow.

NORMA: Maybe not all about it.

JERRY: I hope not.

NORMA: I'd better be going. Dave's got his truck running.

NORMA leaves.

JERRY: Told you so. Now, let me tell you /

GREG enters, interrupting.

GREG: I thought Roy would never stop talking about his videocamera.

MARLENE: Is Andrea still outside?

GREG: She's bagging up plates and cups in the shop.

MARLENE: I'll go give her a hand.

GREG: Don't worry, we've got it. I just wanted to give this to Dad.

GREG pulls a videotape out of his pocket and gives it to JERRY.

JERRY: What's this?

GREG: Roy's tape. The only copy.

JERRY: Thanks, son.

MARLENE: Jerry, you can't destroy that. It's important to the town. The Centennial. Lynda Haverstock.

GREG: Andrea's good with this stuff, Dad. She could delete that…"scene" and leave the rest.

JERRY: That'd be good.

JERRY hands the tape back to GREG.

GREG: I'd better get back to Andrea. Oh, hey, mom, remember that old hanging you were looking for? Andrea had it. She loves it. She dragged me through every art shop in Banff to find a frame for it.

MARLENE: Really? I wonder if I could remember how to make another…

GREG leaves.

JERRY: So this afternoon I /

SUSAN enters without knocking. She looks at her parents.

SUSAN: Oops.

SUSAN backs up, goes back outside, closes the door, and knocks on it.

JERRY: You don't need to knock when Greg and Andrea aren't here.

SUSAN: How would I know who's here if I don't knock?

JERRY: Oh…never mind.

SUSAN: Some kids from Scott's jazz band are drunk out behind the rec centre. We're going to go sort them out. And, Mom—you don't have to keep looking for the green salad bowl.

MARLENE: What?

SUSAN: You left it here. In the basement with some old Tupperware. Andrea set it aside for me. With some of Grandma's china. We both agreed you don't deserve it.

JERRY: They've got you there, Marlene.

SUSAN: So I guess I know where we'll be having Christmas this year.

MARLENE: Oh... Well... I guess if you want to cook...

SUSAN: I might as well, now that I have the green bowl.

JERRY: Never thought I'd eat Christmas turkey in the home of a band teacher.

SUSAN: There's a first time for everything Dad.

SUSAN exits.

JERRY: Christmas with a chihuahua... Maybe we won't be home.

MARLENE: Where else would we be?

JERRY: I've been trying to tell you. I bought that trailer from Norma this afternoon.

MARLENE: What? Really?

JERRY: Yep. We're off to the desert.

MARLENE: Oh Jerry. That would be wonderful.

JERRY: It can't be as dangerous as spring skiing.

MARLENE: I hope the Music Festival board can spare me. And I was thinking of getting some women together to curl. I can't let Norma's rink win playoffs for the third year in a row.

JERRY: Well, we'll see.

MARLENE reaches out to touch JERRY's face.

MARLENE: That cream really did wonders for your face. It's never been so smooth.

Scene 15

Someday, afterwards.

Jerry's shop.

NOTE: This is a nice wrap-up scene, but only if the transition from the previous scene can be made very quickly. If there's going to be a break in the action of more than a couple of seconds, this scene becomes more of an irritation than a resolution, and it would be better to omit this scene from the show. To make the transition quick, JERRY can show a change of season by putting a winter jacket on over his previous outfit.

Loud music is playing. GREG is alone, puttering in his shop, fixing an alternator from a truck or tractor. It's complicated and requires a lot of concentration. GREG grimaces and reaches over to shut the radio off.

GREG: Geez. A guy can't hear himself think with that darn music playing… This alternator is a pain in the neck.

JERRY enters, carrying Tupperware.

JERRY: Brought you and Andrea some of that Norwegian lefse my Grandma used to make. Susan and I've been working on it all day. We're getting pretty good at it.

GREG: Thanks. Do you think you could take a look at this alternator?

JERRY: Nah. I gotta get to town for a meeting. You'll figure it out.

The End.